LIMPING AND WADDLING TO THE REVOLUTION

A MEMOIR OF COLIN BARNETT

BY

RAY MARRIOTT

For a good radical

Colin Barnett

Hayloft Publishing Ltd
South Stainmore
Kirkby Stephen
Cumbria CA17 4DJ

Tel +44 (0) 17683 42300
Fax +44 (0) 17683 41568
Email: books@hayloft.eu
Web: www.hayloft.eu

Printed and bound in the EU

A catalogue record of this book is available from the British Library.

Papers used in this book are made from wood grown in sustainable
forests.

The manufacturing processes conform to EU environmental
regulations.

ISBN-13: 978-1-904-52450-2
ISBN: 1-904-52450-8

For Glenys,

for her love and encouragement

Colin Barnett with his books

CONTENTS

PREFACE

In the 1970s and early 1980s Colin Barnett embodied in the north-west of England everything about the trade union movement that was anathema to successive governments, both Conservative and Labour, and to the tabloid press that supported them. Scarcely a week passed without a sensational report of some industrial outrage in which he played an outspoken and intransigent part. Strikes closed hospitals and care homes and disrupted public services; confrontations between unions and employers dominated the news; and all this against a background of left-wing politics in the region which for a time seemed quite deranged. Indeed Barbara Castle told Colin's future wife that she held him personally responsible for the loss of the 1979 General Election following the "Winter of Discontent".

As the left-wing divisional officer of the fastest-growing public sector union, he was demonised, not only from the right but from the political centre ground as well. And the more he was attacked the more he appeared to thrive on the publicity. Indeed he did much himself to fuel it. The image grew of a militant and determined activist, feared by his opponents and treated warily even by his natural allies. Even twenty years after his retirement, through ill-health, those who remember him still subscribe to the legend of his invincibility and he remains defiantly unapologetic.

I have known him only since his retirement. Had we encountered each other professionally we must have been adversaries. However, the private man is kind and generous, well-read, a supporter of underdogs everywhere and deeply interested in politics and religion. He is also an entertaining companion with a fund of anecdotes.

This memoir is not intended as an *apologia* – no warts have been airbrushed. Rather it is a serious attempt to understand a complex character and to assess a controversial career objectively.

I am grateful to Rodney Bickerstaffe, Derek Gregory and Reg French, former trade union colleagues, for their time and co-operation; to all the former adversaries who have agreed to re-live old battles; to David Boulton and Ian Hamilton Fazey for their journalists' knowledge of events in the north-west; and above all to Colin Barnett himself for his unlimited patience under persistent interrogation.

Ray Marriott
Bishopdale
2007

1. EARLY LIFE

Once, when travelling to attend a meeting in Birmingham, Colin Barnett was recognised instantly by the driver who had been sent to collect him at New Street railway station. Since they had never met previously, he was curious as to how he had been recognised so quickly. The driver replied that he had been told to look out for a "little fat man, limping and waddling".

These characteristics were the legacy of osteomyelitis, a bacterial infection of the bone and bone marrow that had struck him at the age of seven. As a result of a fall from his bike his hip was seriously damaged and he was admitted to Battersea's Bolingbroke Hospital at midnight for emergency treatment. An operation followed to open up his hip and insert bacteria to remove the infected material from his bone marrow, a process which continued for a couple of months. This illness strikes predominantly at children and, seventy years ago, the prognosis for a child with osteomyelitis was bleak, with a very high mortality rate. So the young Barnett was extremely fortunate to survive. One consequence of his illness was enforced hospitalisation for six months. Since the children's ward was closed because of an infection Colin was placed, in traction, on the adult male ward – itself an isolating experience – where, for the first time, he encountered death and serious illness. It also left him with very restricted mobility and, for a while, reliant on callipers to walk. This effectively excluded him from any physical or team activity. Indeed he still recalls his father telling him that he would be ostracized by other children because he was "imperfect". The long-term physical and psychological impact of these events can only be imagined.

Colin was born in 1929 into a family steeped in left-wing politics. His father Arthur was a cold character. He was of Jewish heritage, although he never admitted to that, or that he had changed his name from Levy to Barnett, until near the end of his life. This was perhaps less surprising then, given the anti-Semitism that pervaded Europe in the 1930s and the fear of what fate might befall Jews (and particularly socialist Jews) in the event of a successful German invasion. Barnett (or Barnet) was a name not uncommonly adopted by Jewish immigrants on entry to Britain but Arthur's family were not immigrants. His Jewish ancestry was the result of his grandmother's liaison with a wealthy, married Jewish businessman. Arthur's father (and Colin's grandfather) was therefore illegitimate; he was also apparently the last drover of sheep into Smithfield Market.

At seventeen Arthur had enlisted as a regular soldier in the Royal Horse Artillery in the First World War. However, he was fortunate not to have seen a shot fired in anger as he was posted to the permanent garrison in Jamaica for the duration of the war. After the end of hostilities he had worked as an engineer at the Royal

Arsenal, where he had played a prominent part in the first strike of apprentices. Subsequently he worked as an insurance agent before becoming full-time General Secretary of the Liverpool Victoria Workers Union. He was an active member of the Labour Party and served as Secretary of Putney Constituency Labour Party and delegate to Wandsworth Trades Council. Colin recalls being taken to meetings to hear his father speak but being shocked to discover how inarticulate he was. He was neither a good public speaker nor well educated. Indeed the only book Colin remembers him buying was "Lady Chatterley's Lover", when it was first published by Penguin Books, although he was certainly keen on libraries and is reported to have borrowed up to 8 books per week. In spite of these limitations, however, he was disappointed not to be selected as the Labour parliamentary candidate for Putney in 1945.

Arthur gave very little emotional support to his son. Apart from his cruel and insensitive response to his childhood illness he seems to have found it impossible to offer him any measure of approval. He was a shy and introspective man who found it easier to relate to his son by teasing him. This made Colin uncomfortable in his presence so he avoided bringing home any friends, male or female. He still recalls that it was not until the 1970s, when he was at the height of his powers as an influential trade union official and his widowed father was living temporarily with him and his family at their home in Oldham, that he belatedly expressed some respect for his son's achievements.

Colin's mother, Kathleen, was a harsh parent even by the standards of the 1930s and often resorted to corporal punishment. To her credit, though, when the accepted wisdom was that a child with his physical handicaps belonged in a special school, she insisted that he continue in the local primary school, even when it meant for her a daily journey with a pushchair. She was also his first religious influence. She was a staunch low-church Anglican but, because all the Anglican churches in the immediate neighbourhood had pronounced high church tendencies, she insisted that Colin attend a Methodist chapel.

Many of Colin's earliest recollections are political – hearing the results of the 1935 General Election on the wireless at the age of six; being taken at the age of nine to observe the Mosley riots in the East End; collecting money for Aid to Spain in 1936; and seeing Movietone newsreels of Franco's bombing of Barcelona. He also recalls, at the age of only nine, being taken by his father to observe anti-fascist riots in the East End and seeing people being thrown through shop windows. Clearly these early experiences were a conscious decision on the part of his father, whose judgement in these matters seems to have been less than impressive. But the most influential event in his childhood was the outbreak of the Second World War in 1939.

Like many London children he was an evacuee for almost the complete duration of the war. Initially he was sent to live with his aunt in Littlehampton, where he stayed until 1940, attending a primary school that itself had been evacuated from Tooting. It was here that he won his first (and only) school prize – 10 shillings for speaking for 10 minutes non-stop about London buses. He still recalls that his head teacher expressed incredulity that anyone so young could speak for so long. Clearly the orator's skills were being honed at an early stage in his education. Initially Littlehampton was seen as a considerably safer environment than London but it soon transpired that the Luftwaffe's interest in the coastal towns was almost equally intense, so it was agreed that he would return home to Wandsworth.

Then, at the age of 11, he transferred to secondary school. His father showed little interest in his future schooling but his mother wanted him to have a grammar school education and was apparently unexpectedly assertive with the Headmaster at his interview. Whether it was because or in spite of her tenacity he was accepted into Wandsworth Grammar School in 1940, but by then the school had already been evacuated to Woking, where they shared premises with Woking Grammar School for most of the war. Ironically Woking itself was hardly the ideal refuge either since a factory producing bombers was a close neighbour and an inevitable target for German air raids. Indeed on one such occasion Colin himself was caught in machine-gun fire from an enemy aircraft on his way to school.

At that time Wandsworth was a small, traditional grammar school, led by a distinguished Cambridge scholar, H. Raymond King. King had been appointed in 1932 at the early age of 31. He was a cadaverous-looking man with strong left-wing sympathies. Colin was already marked out as different as a result of his physical disability and massive operation scars as well as what might well have been diagnosed as dyslexia today. So, while other boys took part in physical activities, he had the daily task of collecting the Headmaster's newspapers from W. H. Smith's at Woking station. His instructions were to ensure that the Daily Worker was carefully secreted inside The Times. Many other teachers at the school also had obvious left-wing leanings and Colin now believes that up to half the staff were active or tacit communists! Senior boys were marched off to the cinema to see films supporting the Russian allies and the school was a hot-bed of political debate. The senior boys were sent out to collect aid for Russia and Colin recalls a healthy number of £5 notes slipping into the collecting tins at Woking station. It was also a regular feature of school assemblies to hear a recitation of the names of old boys killed in action or of current pupils killed in the blitz during home visits.

It is tempting to see early evidence of idealism in Colin's decision to join the St John's Ambulance Brigade in preference to the Combined Cadet Force but in truth it was more to do with the commitment to Saturday morning attendance that deterred him from the corps. As part of his St John's duties he was a regular visitor to the Roehampton centre for limbless servicemen and often accompanied the patients to the cinema, where it was normal for him and his charges to be admitted free of charge. He found that, in spite of his own disability, his upper body was strong enough to lift men without legs from their wheelchairs into cinema seats. He also found that, irrespective of his true motives, he gained considerable prestige with the less militarist members of the school staff for being the only St John's volunteer in his year group.

In Woking morning school for the Wandsworth boys took place in local church halls while the resident school occupied the school premises; the Wandsworth pupils were taught in the school buildings in the afternoon. This was a pattern repeated up and down the country where a school in an area considered to be less dangerous hosted a similar school from a more vulnerable area. The evacuated pupils were compulsorily billeted with local families and Colin had a variety of homes during this period. These included the family of a butcher employed at Sainsbury's, who was able to ensure that the boy had considerably more than the normal wartime ration of meat. One of Colin's regular chores was to go to the store to collect a neatly tied (and well-disguised) package containing prime chops and other good cuts of meat for the family table. Only the pregnancy of the butcher's wife intervened to bring this idyllic placement to an end. After this, another temporary home was found for him with a cook, who had worked for a family that had lost their fortune when they were forced to leave Hong Kong as the Japanese invaded.

However these 'postings' were rare highlights in a lonely childhood. Earlier billets had included a soulless hostel, in which Colin was far from happy. This was followed by a squalid council house, where he was so visibly neglected that a shocked billeting officer moved him for a month to a more genteel residence complete with maid and butler, presumably by way of compensation. So eventually in 1944 Colin and his parents decided that life could be no worse for him back in Wandsworth and for the remainder of his secondary school career he moved back to the family home. Unfortunately the school remained in Woking for the duration of the war so Colin then began commuting daily to Woking. But life at home was not noticeably better. Wandsworth was still being bombed with doodle-bugs and he himself suffered health problems, including jaundice, for which he was prescribed an extra allocation of blackcurrant pureé to enhance his intake of vitamin C.

Evacuation had clearly had a pronounced effect on his upbringing and character. Separation from his family served only to reinforce the isolation caused by his handicap and to make him increasingly self-reliant. At a safe distance of over 60 years it is also easy to underestimate the anxieties of a lonely 11 year old, who saw his family only at weekends. During 1940 in Littlehampton he recalls waking up to the sound of church bells, warning of an impending invasion, and worrying about the safety of his parents as he watched a mass of German planes heading for London. Even on home visits family life was scarcely normal. One weekend he and his father left the air-raid shelter in their garden to see what his father predicted would be the "end of London" and a blood-red sky following the bombing of the docks and printing houses. For two days after that he watched black, charred paper falling from the sky.

Only in 1945, following the invasion of France, was the street lighting restored and the school's evacuation to Woking ended. By then Colin had only one further year to complete at school. However, he was becoming actively involved in the Council for Education in World Citizenship (CEWC) and learning a good deal through its activities about the world outside Britain. He recalls that he was the only boy from his school to attend its meetings and remembers booing Max Aitken, who was speaking at Kingsway Hall, because of his sympathetic views on Franco.

At this time he was also introduced to the Anglo-Soviet Youth Friendship Alliance by a young man called Billy Fisher. The organisation was generally seen as subversive and was proscribed by the Labour Party. He recalls that this same Billy Fisher, in spite of his dubious connections, later found employment as a security guard in the Diplomatic Service and was subsequently imprisoned for spying for Russia from his position in the British Embassy in Moscow.

The home to which Colin had returned in 1944 was now once more engaged in domestic politics. The national unity that had been generated during the war effort was still much in evidence but now the mood was one of optimism and all the talk was of reconstruction and social change. Colin's father canvassed actively for the Labour Party in the July 1945 election while Colin was allowed the day off from school to knock up voters in Woking. He recalls seeing Edith Summerskill canvassing in Putney, where she was to become the new Labour MP, and taking part in the booing of Churchill, the national saviour, simply because he was a Tory. Since many of the voters were still abroad in the armed services, three weeks were allowed for votes to be cast and it took six weeks for the results to be announced; and, when they were, he may well have been the youngest person present at the Labour Party victory celebrations in Westminster Hall and joined enthusiastically in singing the 'Red Flag' in Downing Street.

The election result was overwhelming. With an overall majority of 146 the Labour Party had taken 210 seats from the Conservatives and won 79 seats that had never before returned a Labour member. The total Labour vote had increased from just over 8 million at the previous election, which had taken place as long ago as ten years previously in 1935, to 12 million in 1945. In London the number of Labour MPs increased from 27 to 49. If the extent of the Labour victory had surprised many commentators it soon became clear that the Tories, far from basking in the sunlight of victory in the war, were paying the price for their pre-war policies. Moreover the electorate were attempting to put the war behind them and looking forward to the fruits of peace.

Attlee, as Deputy Prime Minister in the wartime government, had spent most of his time planning the post-war reconstruction while Churchill concentrated his energies on winning the war. Many, if not most, of the ministers wielding power on the home front in the wartime coalition had also been key Labour personalities. In addition to Attlee himself, Morrison had been Home

Secretary, Bevin Minister of Labour and Dalton President of the Board of Trade. Clearly the new Labour government was both well-prepared for the task in hand and thoroughly experienced. So in spite of the crushing financial burden of waging a long war and the consequent reliance on the United States for economic support, the expectations of the electorate were high on the domestic front. It was therefore the most natural thing for an idealistic young man from a socialist family to join the Labour Party as soon as he was old enough.

There seems to have been no expectation that Colin would pursue further academic study beyond matriculation, though there is little doubt that he would have been well capable of pursuing an academic sixth-form course. So, by the time he left school at 16, this disabled, dyslexic and solitary lad had immersed himself in the left-wing politics of both his relatively uneducated father and his intellectually stimulating teachers, from whom he had acquired a rosy picture of the gallant Russian allies; he had experienced at first hand the ravaging effects of a highly mechanised war and had adopted a pacifist creed; and he had developed an avid interest in reading, which was to mould his political philosophy and religious beliefs for the rest of his life.

2. INTO WORK

The young Barnett's first job after matriculation in 1946 was with Barclays Bank, in Victoria Street, SW1. On his very first pay-day he joined the Fabian Society, whose headquarters were just around the corner from the bank. His first question on taking up his very junior post in the bank was to ask how to join the union - the Bank Officers Guild. Scarcely a hot-bed of revolutionary socialism, nonetheless the union was treated with some suspicion by the managerial grades. There can therefore be little surprise that Colin was considered not to have a rosy future in the rather staid and traditional banking world and that his first job lasted just 3 months.

His next foray into gainful employment was as a library assistant at the London School of Economics, where he stayed quite blissfully for 5 years. Naturally he joined a union and discovered that this was entirely more acceptable behaviour at the LSE than at Barclays. Even if the ready availability of an impressive book stock had been insufficient incentive, access to the lectures of such impressive intellectuals of the left as Harold Laski and R. H. Tawney would surely have convinced him that he had found his niche. Both were at the height of their powers.

Tawney had been on the staff of the LSE since 1912 and

had been appointed Professor of Economic History in 1931. He was pre-eminent among socialist academics and influenced generations of liberal-minded students. He also espoused the expansion of educational opportunity and for over forty years was prominent in the Workers Education Association. As a Christian and a Socialist it is not difficult to see why the young Barnett should find his ideas so enticing.

Three of Tawney's many written works were among the most influential of their time. "The Acquisitive Society" (1926) argued strongly that material acquisitiveness was both morally wrong and socially corrupting. "Religion and the Rise of Capitalism" (1926) examined the relationship between religion and social, economic and political developments in the sixteenth and seventeenth centuries that led to the rise of capitalism. "Equality" (1931) was concerned mainly with social and economic inequality and was a strong influence in the formation of Labour Party policy.

Laski was another major influence on Labour party thinking. He was Professor of Political Science at the LSE from 1926 to 1950 with a brilliant international reputation. He was also a member of Labour's National Executive from 1937 to 1949, during which time he played a prominent part in the creation of the manifesto for the 1945 General Election.

Colin recalls that he often spoke with Tawney and attended Laski's lectures on the British constitution, which more often than not were a re-run of what had transpired at the most recent meeting of the Labour Party National Executive. In these reports he was particularly severe on Ernest Bevin, whom he regarded with disdain because of his pro-Arab sympathies. In fact Colin spent so much time and energy as a pseudo-student, attending lectures and meetings of the Communist and Socialist societies and Student Christian Movement (SCM), that it was fortunate that he was distinctly under-employed first as a library assistant and then on promotion to the information desk.

The SCM at the LSE was at that time oriented very much to the left and Colin became its Vice-President. It was in these meetings that he first met John Stonehouse, the future Postmaster-General, whose subsequent disappearing act and imprisonment for fraud made him more of a household name than his modest political career would ever have ensured. He also became close to Peter Archer (Solicitor-General 1974-79) who, he recalls, even then entertained strong ambitions to become Chancellor of the Exchequer.

So by this time religion, which his mother had always encouraged him to take part in, had become a significant part of Colin's life. She had steered him strongly towards Methodism, which he found sat comfortably with his socialism. At the same time his father, who was far less interested in any of the more positive aspects of religion, shared his wife's antipathy to high church influences and especially those of the Roman Catholic Church. In fact Arthur seems to have entertained real fears of Roman Catholicism, warning his young son at one stage about the danger of being kidnapped by nuns! Colin himself had become far more suspicious of Catholicism since learning of that church's support for Franco in Spain and its ambivalence towards the German Nazis. Indeed the more he read of German history the more amazed he became at the power of religion in politics.

It appears with hindsight that the part played by religion in his formative years was mainly to underpin his political beliefs, particularly as the euphoria of the Labour victory in 1945 gave way to a more brutal realism and disappointment. The financial millstone of the war, together with the loss of export markets and the substantial damage to the merchant fleet, all conspired to undermine the government's economic ambitions. Post-war loans from the USA and Canada soon ran out. The winter of 1946-47 was the worst since 1880-81 and so severe that it seriously damaged the coal industry and led to a fuel crisis.

In Parliament, however, there was an unprecedented programme of legislation including the establishment of the National Health Service, extensive new housing and the reorganisation of the planning system, as well as an ambitious programme of nationalisation. These foundations of the welfare state were greeted enthusiastically by those who had fought for a Labour victory in 1945.

By 1950, however, the combined impact of financial crises, devaluation and legislative exhaustion had taken their toll and, in spite of all the government's reforms, the prevailing mood among those who had pinned their hopes on Attlee to achieve nothing less than the transformation of society was one of disappointment. In effect they had run out of steam. In addition the party had effectively disadvantaged itself through the redistribution of parliamentary seats under the Representation of the People Act. This was reflected in the results of the 1950 General Election with a swing to the Conservatives of 3.3% and a reduction in the overall Labour majority to only 5. So, at the opening of the new Parliament, the Government felt able to propose only minor measures. This was not a position that could be sustained for a whole parliament and, in the election which followed quickly afterwards in 1951, the Conservatives were back in power with an overall majority of 17. The Labour legacy was impressive but many of the activists in the Party were disillusioned and considered that an even greater opportunity had been lost.

Perhaps this political disappointment, which Colin was to experience many times in the next 50 years, was in part responsible for his new quest for social improvement through religion. With the Labour Party in the political equivalent of the convalescent home and the Conservatives securely in power for at least another five years, it is difficult to see where else a committed socialist might turn. He now also began to take a deeper interest in theology, seeking perhaps in the church to reinforce the unwavering certainties of his political beliefs. However, his religious quest was always to prove less successful for him as, the more he read, the more elusive he found the certain truths that he sought.

Still, these were early days in his religious journey and his next job was as an administrative assistant to the campaigning Methodist minister, Rev Donald Soper, in his work with the Order of Christian Witness. Although the work was administrative he began to discover more about the reality of poverty through visits to probation hostels and working with down-and-outs in London. The link between religion and socialist politics thus grew ever stronger in his life. Soper himself was an extremely gifted public speaker and, through his "soap-box" sessions at Hyde Park Corner (Sundays) and Tower Hill (Wednesdays), inspired Colin to develop his own skills as an orator.

Soper, the Superintendent of the West London Mission, was ardently opposed to capitalism, the arms trade, gambling, alcohol and blood-sports and, in spite of being brought up in a Liberal family, was an active member of the Labour Party. His experience of social deprivation in his early ministry in Derby and London had converted him to socialism and he was especially concerned to explore the political implications of the Christian gospel. He was also a pacifist who was a member first of the Peace Pledge Union and subsequently of the Campaign for Nuclear Disarmament. Indeed he was so persuasive an advocate for pacifism that he was banned from the airwaves by the BBC for the duration of the Second World War.

It was during Colin's work with Soper that the Korean

War began. Having so recently seen off the threat of the extreme right in Europe, the new prospect of an armed conflict with eastern communists presented British socialists with a major dilemma, as the government they had worked so hard to put in power became embroiled in a war for which they had little sympathy. Colin's principal reaction to the war was as a pacifist and he became involved with the 'Peace with China' movement, along with many other left-wing Christians. This theme would be a constant in his life and would bring him into contact with other influential pacifists and the Campaign for Nuclear Disarmament as well as encouraging him to work for closer cultural links with Russia in the pursuit of international understanding and friendship.

He began also to seek to link his religion and politics more actively in society. He became involved with the Society of Methodist Clergy and also developed an interest in the French concept of "worker priests". That movement arose from the Roman Catholic Church's concern early in the twentieth century at their inability to connect with industrial workers. There had been a number of experimental approaches designed to bring priests closer to the working lives of the working classes but the key initiative was that of Father Jacques Loew, sent by the Dominicans to live among the dockworkers of Marseilles. The initial intention was that he should study the conditions of the working classes but Loew felt that he could do this more effectively by becoming one of them and taking up manual work in the dockyards. Other priests followed his example and the movement became established in Paris as well.

However, the hierarchy of the Catholic Church became seriously concerned about this initiative by the early 1950s. Of almost 150 worker-priests, 20 had married and left the Church altogether; of those that remained many had joined unions that had Communists affiliations and had begun to participate in left-wing politics. Even without this politicisation of their role the Vatican had become worried that their secular work was diverting their attention into worldly pursuits. So in 1954 Pius XII effectively brought the experiment to an end. However, many priests, including Loew, continued to minister to the workers through the development of "industrial missions".

In Britain Leslie Hunter, Bishop of Sheffield from 1939 to 1962, was not a supporter of French-style "worker priests" and actually opposed attempts to develop similar approaches in the Anglican Church. However, Hunter was attempting to develop the "industrial mission" concept, which Colin found attractive, and the young man was considering seriously the possibility of being ordained into the Anglican Church in order to pursue his interest.

He particularly admired clerics such as the charismatic Mervyn Stockwood, to whom he was given an introduction by his sister-in-law, who was working as a youth worker in Bristol. In due course Colin visited Stockwood at St Mary's, Bristol. In addition to his pastoral duties Stockwood was also a Labour councillor and the Chairman of the Housing Committee in Bristol.

He advised Colin on appropriate reading to explore the "worker priest" concept more thoroughly. Stockwood also warned him to reflect carefully on the differences between Britain and France; across the Channel there was a stronger tradition of clerics working directly with the less privileged and the unemployed, whereas in Britain the churches and unions alike trod more carefully, since it seemed that no one had the stomach for any initiative that might foster a mass movement of the unemployed.

Stockwood also suggested that he visit the Reverend Ted Wickham, Director of the Sheffield Industrial Mission, which was the first of its kind in the country. Wickham had founded the Mission in 1944. Its role was to address the progressive estrangement of the working classes from organised religion, which had so affected the membership of the church in the urban areas since the Industrial Revolution. He and his chaplains sought to engage with the working population of Sheffield by visiting steelworks and other heavy industries and involving the workers during their breaks in formal discussions about issues of importance to them. The Sheffield Industrial Mission enjoyed enormous support from Bishop Hunter and in the 1950s was serving as a model for similar developments elsewhere in British industrial towns and cities.

So, in 1955, as a result of his discussions with Stockwood, this serious and cerebral young man, who had never seen the industrial north of England and whose movements were still significantly handicapped from his childhood illness, decided to take a manual job in the steelworks of Sheffield and see whether the "worker priest" model might be right for him. For two years he worked hard, rolling and cleaning stainless steel in the rolling mills, which he described as a "Dante's Inferno" with scant regard for health and safety.

Hard as the work was, it left plenty of time for reading and he was able to combine his employment with a growing involvement in the industrial mission as a possible prelude to ordination. He also discovered for the first time the solidarity of the working classes when fellow-workers, who must have been bemused to discover this well-read, well-spoken but severely handicapped Londoner sharing their work, arranged for their wives to knit scarves for him to reduce the chafing on his neck.

However, it is apparent that his more extreme left-wing views and a burgeoning interest in South American 'liberation theology' sat somewhat uneasily with the generally orthodox socialist attitudes then prevailing in the mission, which was incidentally proving very influential in the upper ranks of the Labour Party nationally. Not for the last time in his life Colin was proving to be something of a political misfit.

In 1953, before his move to Sheffield, Colin had married his first wife, Margaret, a teacher whom he had met in London. She was clearly in sympathy with his political interests and became involved in the same political groups. It was not uncommon to find Colin establishing a power base by serving as the secretary of any organisation he belonged to and for Margaret to be listed as "assistant secretary". She obtained a teaching post in Sheffield, where a more outward-looking attitude was apparent than in some northern towns at that time, where employment as a teacher had more to do with a local upbringing and contacts than with professional ability.

Indeed the mid-1950s were heady days in Sheffield. The communist-fronted World Peace Council, under pressure from the CIA, had recently decamped from Europe to Sheffield and the left-wing City Council was not unsympathetic to the cause. Colin continued his involvement with the "Peace with China" campaign which staged large-scale public meetings and demonstrations and attracted influential speakers such as A.J.P. Taylor, the eminent and controversial historian, and Aneurin Bevan MP, all of whom gave their services free of charge. At one such meeting advance warning of a violent right-wing demonstration caused enormous consternation, when it was realised that all the stewards at the meeting were Quakers and therefore unlikely to intervene physically. Fortunately, enough of the local police contingent had sufficient recent and personal experience of fighting fascism in Europe to make them ready and more than adequate replacements in dealing with the Sheffield far-right. The incursion was dispersed with relatively little trouble.

Sheffield was also a centre of campaigning against nuclear testing, partly on political grounds but also out of concern about the safety of air tests and Strontium 90.

Colin himself was the founder and secretary of the Sheffield Campaign against Nuclear Tests. Indeed in June 1958 he found himself with a three-minute slot to practise his oratorical skills at a rally in Trafalgar Square, where other speakers included Canon John Collins, Rev. Donald Soper and Michael Foot MP. Even today Colin still regards the ultimately successful fight against nuclear testing as one of the most significant achievements of his life.

Most of the prominent church figures in Sheffield were active in the group and, at one stage, fearing suppression of their activities and removal of their records, Colin arranged to have them stored more securely in Bishop Hunter's safe, an arrangement with which Hunter was apparently entirely comfortable. At one stage some forty clergymen (including the Archdeacon) and ministers in the Sheffield District signed the policy statement of the Sheffield Campaign for Nuclear Disarmament.

A major figure in both religion and left-wing politics in Sheffield at the time was Canon Alan Eccleston. Intriguingly, however, he was married to the daughter of the Bishop of Carlisle, who herself had been brought up at Chatsworth House and was related to six members of the Conservative government. He was a gentle and erudite man who was known at the time as "the second most brilliant man in the Church of England". He was also Secretary of the local Communist party. No doubt he also sympathised strongly with the objectives of CND but the movement was wary of becoming involved too closely with a man who had such overt Communist sympathies. Other clerics involved in the same movement and who had a major influence on Colin at this time were Ted Wickham, who was also later to become Bishop of Middleton (in Manchester), and Alfred Jowett, Vicar of St George's Sheffield and later Dean of Manchester. Indeed it was in Jowett's front room that many of the key meetings of left-wing sympathisers took place in Sheffield.

Colin himself became a diocesan representative in the House of Laity of the Church Assembly. No one previously had sought election by means of a 'manifesto' but this did not deter him. In his statement to the members of the Diocesan Conference he wrote:-

"I wish to offer myself as a candidate for election to the House of Laity of the Church Assembly. As I am unknown to many of you, may I submit details of my experience.

"I am a loyal and convinced member of the Church of England without holding any party allegiance.

"My main concern is with the mission of the Church in an industrial society and the role that the layman has to play in that mission.

"Prior to living in Sheffield I had two years' experience of mission work. Before commencing my present work in the Welfare Department of the Education Office I gained some experience of industrial life by working as a labourer in a large steel works.

"The experience I have gained in an Industrial Parish and with the Sheffield Industrial Mission convinces me that the Church must concern itself with all major questions of the day if it is to progress.

"My work has also taught me that we must take all problems of ecumenical co-operation seriously, particularly in regard to the future of the Church of South India."

The use of the words "party allegiance" presumably referred to factions within the Church since his secular political affiliations must by now have been all too apparent to the citizens of Sheffield. In any event his "manifesto" (which was also the first of many in his own career!) proved strikingly popular and, with the support of the Bishop behind the scenes, he topped the poll.

The Church Assembly met in Church House, Westminster and there he rubbed shoulders with many more interesting characters who identified with left-wing causes, including Mary Hardcastle, then Principal of Charlotte Mason College in Cumbria. It was while sitting next to her one day that he made an impassioned speech denouncing the Prime Minister, Harold Macmillan, only to be tackled by another member, who was the Prime Minister's brother and a High Court judge, who warned him seriously about the laws of slander!

By this time, although his interest in the church as a layman had not diminished, Colin's flirtation with combining manual work and ordination appears to have been over. The physical strain of the rolling mills had taken its toll and he had, in any case, concluded that the interests of low-paid and unemployed people would be better served through the trade union movement than through the structures of the church.

To further this plan he therefore left the steel mills for a clerical post in the Sheffield City Council education department. He worked his way through various sections of the department, working on further education awards, education welfare, the school health service and admissions to residential special schools, before being promoted to the planning department. New to the local government service, he joined the Municipal Officers Guild, a semi-autonomous union which later became part of NALGO.

However, it was around this time that he first became interested in the National Union of Public Employees, an altogether more dynamic and radical organisation and far more in tune with his left-wing beliefs. So, within a year, he transferred his allegiance to NUPE. It was then but a short time before he became Branch Secretary (naturally!), where he found himself much closer to the political heart of the City Council, often to the annoyance of his own chief officer, particularly when he was summoned to private meetings with the Chairman of the Education Committee. Gradually the realisation dawned on him that, however devout the intention, without political power there was little to be achieved in improving society and he found in NUPE the ideal organ for his views.

3. THE NATIONAL UNION OF PUBLIC EMPLOYEES (NUPE)

For an active man of the left in the 1950s there could scarcely have been a more congenial home in the whole of British trade unionism. NUPE had its roots in the steady growth of municipal services in the late-Victorian era. In the more progressive urban areas municipal enterprise was regarded as an expression of civic pride, reflected in many of the impressive town halls and other public buildings constructed in this period. In other areas, however, civic parsimony was perhaps a more apt description, where fidelity to the interests of the ratepayer largely over-rode the perceived need for expanded public services to help the needy. In these areas municipal workers were not as well treated and the lowest pay was to be found, particularly in the rural areas, where far more use was made of "contracting out" in preference to the direct employment of labour.

It was against this background that municipal trade unions began to form in the late 1880s, initially in London. Their main role then was providing limited financial benefits (especially upon death) to their members, following the earlier model of the friendly societies, and campaigning for better pay and conditions. They were particularly opposed to the contracting out of services although they had not yet embarked upon strike action as a campaigning tool.

By 1891 the London County Council had 3000 employees in membership of the Vestry Employees Union. As the new unions became better organised they took up the cudgels for better pay and conditions rather more assertively. The employers saw the need for stout resistance to these demands and to drive down costs and it was not long before the first municipal strikes were seen. As membership of these unions grew, they were treated with much suspicion by both the TUC and the Labour Party, who saw separate unions for municipal workers as potentially divisive in a movement that was traditionally national and craft-based.

When NUPE was formed in 1928 it had a membership of about 12,500 and could trace its history successively through the National Municipal Labour Union, the Municipal Employees Association and the National Union of Corporation Workers. But this was not a time for faint hearts. During the General Strike many public sector workers had undertaken secondary action in support of the miners and the government had responded in 1927 with legislation in the form of the Trades Disputes and Trades Unions Act, which limited the scope of industrial action that could be taken by public workers. Indeed the Act exposed public sector workers to prosecution for breach of contract if they failed to provide services through taking strike action. It also prohibited local and public authorities from making trade union membership a condition of employment. Since this was also a period of cuts in public sector wages, the combined result of these measures was greatly increased financial pressure on the unions themselves. So it was something of a triumph for the NUCW to have held its membership constant at around 12,000 throughout the mid-1920s.

The second General Secretary of the NUCW and the first of NUPE was Jack Wills, the former secretary of the Building Workers Industrial Union. It fell to him to restructure the union to meet the new financial and legal environment. With the Local Government Act 1929, which transferred former Poor Law workers to the employment of local authorities, came many challenges to the unions representing them, as conditions of service and pension rights came under attack. NUPE was particularly aggressive in this struggle and the publicity generated by these efforts also attracted extra members, often from among the ranks of other public sector unions. This buccaneering attitude did little to endear NUPE to the other unions and for many years its leaders were ostracised within the TUC, failing to gain the representation on negotiating bodies and seats on the General Council which the union's numerical size clearly warranted. At this stage in its development NUPE was subsequently to be described by Aneurin Bevan as "nearly extinct".

On the death of Jack Wills, the 36 year-old Bryn Roberts, a Welsh Methodist from Abertillery, was appointed

General Secretary, serving from 1934 to 1962. A former miner and a conscientious objector, who was a close friend of Bevan and had been imprisoned for refusing conscription during the First World War, Roberts had a rather dapper appearance, wearing wing-collars in contrast to the traditional cloth-cap image presented by other union leaders. Throughout his career he stood outside the conservative trade union establishment and did not shrink from controversy. In 1934 he found himself and his "nearly extinct" union excluded from all national negotiating committees. It still had only 13,000 members in 122 branches and what W.W. Craik described in his biography of Bryn Roberts as a "toilsome and troublesome history behind it".

Roberts came to NUPE with a long-term plan to expand the membership, which was undoubtedly his most important contribution over the next 28 years. Many of the early campaigns were designed to improve the pay of county council roadmen and in this they eventually enjoyed considerable success, but only after many reverses. They were less successful before the war in extending their membership to school caretakers. Nor did they make much headway with workers in hospitals, but these were struggles to which they would return in the post-war years following the Butler Education Act and the formation of the National Health Service; and Colin Barnett was to play a significant role in them.

It was only Roberts' success during the Second World War in organising the Auxiliary Fire Service (AFS) and the ARPs that finally brought him greater acceptance after the war, together with a place on national negotiating committees. The union's agreement after the war to sanction the transfer of all the AFS members to the Fire Brigades Union also won friends for NUPE in that union and the relationship between the two organisations remained close in the ensuing years.

Roberts remorselessly championed the low paid and the unemployed and was one of the early proponents of a national minimum wage and a single public service union, to both of which most other unions remained implacably opposed, as did the Labour Party for many years. Fear of a minimum wage arose because it was seen as undermining free collective bargaining and, at a time of skill shortages, those unions serving the skilled workers simply did not want to be fettered in any way. NUPE, on the other hand, had very few skilled workers in its membership and little with which to trade on the labour market.

NUPE and its controversial General Secretary were hated by the more conservative barons of the rival public sector unions, the Transport and General Workers Union and the General Municipal and Boilermakers Union and they both used their influence in the TUC to limit that of NUPE. However, these unions were almost entirely urban-based and one of the reasons for the successful and rapid expansion of NUPE's membership during and after the Roberts era was NUPE's concentration on the recruitment of public sector manual workers in the previously unorganised rural areas. The downside of this strategy of course was that the employers in rural areas required far more persuasion than their counterparts in the towns and cities to accept the unionisation of their workforces. It also involved the union's officers in a great deal of travel.

When Bryn Roberts moved a resolution at the 1946 Trade Union Congress in support of "one all-embracing National Joint Industrial Council" to replace the myriad of separate industrial councils operating in local government, it was defeated by 3,763,000 votes to 2,173,000 at the instigation of the other general unions, who saw in this approach a real threat to their own positions. Given NUPE's impoverished situation in 1934 it is remarkable that by 1946 their General Secretary could muster even as many as 2 million votes for such a controversial proposal. This degree of progress was a mark of Roberts' determination and the growth in the influence of his union.

However, his philosophy and his methods were anathema to more conservative unionists. For example, he had little time for the "Bridlington Agreement" which since 1939 had regulated the movement of members between unions – effectively creating a cartel. His belief was either that competitive unionism should be ended by creating single unions for single industries and services or that competition between unions should be allowed to operate without restriction. In short, members should be permitted to choose which union they belonged to, not vice versa. In Roberts' own words:

"Were it not for those totalitarian regulations, thousands

of public employees, who are now, against their wishes, tied to the other and particularly general unions, would join NUPE's forces and this Union would soon become the one and only union representative of those employed in the local government and health service, which is this Union's objective."

Now these were the official views of NUPE, not just of Roberts personally, but the trade union movement appeared to hold Roberts entirely responsible for them and punished him accordingly. Throughout his period of office he was denied the place on the TUC General Council to which his abilities and the numerical strength of his union would appear to have entitled him. Yet, after Roberts' retirement in 1962, it was but a short time before his successor Sydney Hill was elected to the Council without being required to recant any of Roberts' policies. The antipathy to Roberts was clearly personal. So it is small wonder that this maverick, who was the inspiration behind the expansion of NUPE for over three decades, was also the beacon which drew an increasingly unorthodox Colin Barnett into the union's full-time employment.

During his time in Sheffield Colin had become convinced that he wanted to work as a full-time union officer. He saw it as a route to greater power and influence to be used to the benefit of the low-paid and unemployed and felt ideologically committed to the principles of NUPE. So, when he saw in "Tribune" an advertisement for a full-time post of "Assistant Organiser in the Nottinghamshire Area", he applied and was offered an interview before the entire National Executive.

His preparation, as usual, was meticulous and included reading "Bryn Roberts and the National Union of Public Employees", a less than critical biography by W W Craik, which had been published in 1955. He also took the opportunity to impress Roberts with the national contacts he had already made, particularly through his church activities. For example, he had already struck up a friendly relationship with Bishop Bell of Chichester, who had become an honorary member of NUPE for his support for the low-paid. At the beginning of his interview it was noted that he had previously worked for Rev Donald Soper and he was somewhat surprised to be asked if he would like to lead the Executive in prayer!

In spite of his willingness do so, he was not successful in his interview but he obviously made a positive impact on the NUPE hierarchy because the minute of the appointing committee reads:-

"It was recommended unanimously that Mr Michael J. Watson be appointed on the usual probationary terms but that the General Secretary write to Mr Colin M. Barnett informing him that the Union would give earnest consideration to any application he might make when a vacancy occurred in the Yorkshire Area."

A nod from the all-powerful National Executive was as good as the proverbial wink and in 1960 Colin found himself appointed as a full-time union official in

Yorkshire in a union whose membership was now in excess of 200,000. This growth in membership was allowing NUPE to recruit additional officers and the new breed, of which Colin was perhaps the most forthright example, were a more inspired and exciting bunch, quite prepared to overturn conventions and cock a snook at the trade union establishment. That they were also to some extent class warriors must also have made them risky appointments and a challenge to any manager. Their priority was in every case to expand the union's membership. On his appointment Roberts gave Colin a second copy of Craik's biography, leading him to boast that he was probably the only man in England who possessed two copies and, judging from its hagiographical approach, perhaps the only one with the stamina to read the entire book!

Already a sick man when he retired in 1962, Bryn Roberts died only two years later in 1964. At a memorial meeting held to celebrate his life and work, Vic Feather, then the Assistant General Secretary of the TUC, said:-

"Many of the things that Bryn spoke about at Congress years ago are accepted by the trade union movement today as though they have never been different. But other ideas that Bryn mooted twenty years ago and more are only now coming up as subjects for discussion .... His approach was always a frontal attack, a trumpet blast, a march, and every banner flying. The impact of all this effervescence was often disturbing. It was not because he was misunderstood; Bryn spoke too clearly and trenchantly to be

misunderstood. It was disturbing because he meant it to be."

It is not too difficult to discern in this tribute the essence of the man who was the role model for NUPE's latest recruit to its full-time staff.

4. THE UNION MAN

Colin's first post in NUPE was as an "assistant organiser" for the Leeds Division. Although he worked as part of the team employed in the Leeds office in Blenheim Terrace, he was actually based in Harrogate, where he also set up home. Harrogate itself was not a promising battle-ground for a class warrior and active socialist - not even a Christian socialist. Before the war the Union of Fascists had found considerable sympathy there and there was a strong undercurrent of anti-semitism still evident after the war.

The Labour Party in Harrogate was very much a minority group and, within two days of moving there, Colin found himself elected as secretary (again) of the constituency party. He was also instrumental in forming the "Harrogate Left Club", described as a "forum for socialist discussion and activities to which all Harrogate and Knaresborough socialists will be welcome". It is hard to imagine that their membership was huge. Such was the pre-occupation with politics and trade union affairs in the Barnett household that, on starting primary school in Harrogate, his son Ian distinguished himself by demanding to know to which union the head teacher belonged!

The practical difficulties of covering a large rural patch soon became obvious. Colin was not yet able to drive a car so initially his journeys all had to be made either by public transport or on a BSA Bantam motorcycle. Clearly this could not continue for very long, so driving lessons were quickly arranged. One former colleague, who had initially taken him under his wing and was familiar with Colin's modest driving skills, accompanied him to his driving test in Barnsley. Nearly 50 years later his colleague still recalls with some amazement that he managed to pass the test; an achievement that seems to have had more to do with the examiner's mind being on his wife's birthday than the learner's actual performance. By all accounts the space allowed for the usually problematical three-point turn would have been sufficient for a modern jumbo jet. Success in the driving test also brought a NUPE standard-issue Ford Popular into the equation and travel became considerably simpler after that, even if the early Popular found it impossible to climb hills and operate its windscreen wipers at the same time.

The Divisional Officer in Yorkshire at that time was Wilf Window who was soon impressed with Colin's work-rate. Window had served in both wars, entering the army as a 14 year-old volunteer, becoming a commissioned officer, and rising finally to the rank of captain in 1945. He cut an impressive figure with the rural roadmen, many of whom were themselves ex-servicemen and his status also gave him a useful entrée with the County Surveyors, many of whom in the immediate post-war period were ex-senior officers in the

Royal Engineers. Every small advantage had to be used to best effect in the battle for recognition and new members and branches and Captain Window made the most of his previous position.

Even so, the resistance which the union encountered, especially in the more conservative rural areas, was palpable. The Clerk to the East Riding County Council, for example, could not abide trade unions and, when he was finally obliged to meet Colin, he refused to offer him even a cup of tea from his silver tray, in spite of the fact that he had driven all the way from Harrogate to Beverley for the meeting. The arrival of the tray, it seems, was traditionally the tacit signal for the end of the meeting. Now Colin Barnett has always been both resourceful and bloody-minded and certainly slow to take a hint so, at his next meeting with the august Clerk, he took with him a battered thermos flask and poured his own coffee when the silver tray appeared. Apparently the Clerk was less than gracious in this small defeat.

The old rural district councils were perhaps the most resistant to trade union activity. At a meeting at one such council he had to resort to stamping his feet before he could have an audience, while in Boston, Lincolnshire, the Hospital Secretary boasted to his face that she always tore his letters up. However, attitudes changed in there at least when Colin's insistence in a grievance hearing that specialist medical advice be sought before a final decision was taken resulted in the diagnosis of an otherwise unrecognised brain tumour and the saving of a NUPE member's life. A similar spark of intuition achieved a similar result later on in the Lancashire Ambulance Service. Elsewhere in Lincolnshire, he recalls beginning an address to an appeal panel in Sleaford with the usual "ladies and gentlemen" only to be pulled up immediately by the chairman and informed that he should have referred to "lords, ladies and gentlemen".

Colin's principal union responsibilities in Yorkshire were in the field of recruitment. It had become clear to the union hierarchy that many of the lower-paid (and often part-time) public sector workers had still to join a trade union and the competition for their signatures was immense, though less so in the rural areas where NUPE had a definite edge. In addition to the accepted advantages to the employee of having the support and protection of a union there was also the financial and political clout that increased membership gave to the union concerned.

So recruitment had become the highest priority for Bryn Roberts and Colin found he had a real talent for it. In his first week in Leeds he processed fifty new membership applications, although the fact that they were all outstanding applications from potential members known to him in Sheffield appears to have gone largely unnoticed. However, when he turned his attention to the porters and other domestic staff at Leeds University, which was located just across the road from the NUPE office, his score soon passed the 700 mark. This success was all the sweeter since the university was also just across the road from the TGWU office and they had apparently made little or no effort to establish themselves there.

These achievements were not due exclusively to Colin's own direct efforts for he managed also to secure the support and co-operation of influential figures within the university. These included Ralph Miliband and John Rex, two left-wing lecturers, as well as Agnes Patrick from the administrative staff and Mary Ringsleben, who was a leading figure in CND and for whom Colin at one time exercised power of attorney while she was in prison as a consequence of demonstrating at a nuclear site in the Doncaster area. Even the Vice-Chancellor, whose wife was actually a NUPE member in her own right, gave help and succour to the recruitment campaign. Averil Barr, a former colleague of Colin's in the Student Christian Movement at the London School of Economics, had become secretary to the Vice-Chancellor and proved extremely helpful, often passing on advice from the Vice-Chancellor about what might (and might not) be acceptable to the university in pay negotiations.

His first victory in Leeds University was to obtain holiday pay for his members. With such left-wing sympathies among the academic staff (who themselves enjoyed the benefit of holiday pay and many other advantages) it is perhaps surprising that this small concession had not already been extended to the lower paid without the necessity for union intervention. However, Colin's observation was that the academic staff were generally ignorant of the manual staff's conditions of service and that they were not at all reluctant to rectify the problem once it was pointed out to them.

There is plenty of evidence therefore, even at this stage in his career, of Colin's networking skills, especially among the educated and academic adherents of the Left. He also soon found himself nominated in Selby as a Labour candidate for a West Riding County Council election, while his wife contested a seat in Harrogate – more, one suspects, as a noble and loyal gesture than a realistic bid for a career in local politics. Neither was elected. However, the Labour-controlled West Riding County Council did nominate him as a governor of Sedbergh School soon afterwards. Then, as now, this was an independent school without any strong left-wing inclinations, so the honour of his nomination was short-lived as the governing body rejected him – a decision of which their successors have no doubt been reminded since his retirement to live in Sedbergh.

His sojourn in Yorkshire was for only two years and he appears to have made his mark on the local scene sufficiently for the local newspaper in Harrogate to have remarked somewhat gracelessly that his departure in 1962 for the East Midlands was "Harrogate's gain".

His second posting was not actually a promotion because that was not altogether how things worked in NUPE in the 1960s. When the call came the loyal union man, just like his equivalent in holy orders, was expected to respond without question, without a pay rise and usually without so much as his removal expenses or legal fees. The Midlands Regional Office was located in Birmingham but, since the rapid growth in membership also warranted the appointment of additional full-time staff, there were now sufficient members in the East Midlands area to justify a new office in Nottingham.

One colleague who visited him in the East Midlands recalls that he seemed "ill at ease", speaking with the rapidity of a machine gun as a cover for his natural shyness. He had no small talk at all and was seen as an aloof if not lonely figure, driven entirely by the demands of the job and quite uninterested in establishing personal relationships with his colleagues.

His brief in Nottingham was to develop the work he had started in the recruitment of new members but also, in the light of his experience in Leeds, to concentrate his energies nationally on recruitment in the rapidly expanding higher education sector, which was very largely virgin territory. The campaign to recruit members in the universities had already been adopted by NUPE as a national priority and, throughout the early 1960s, university ancillary and technical staff joined NUPE in large numbers, particularly from the newer institutions and from universities like Leeds where there was sympathetic support among the academic staff.

In addition to Leeds, Colin's successes in the university sector included establishing new branches in Sheffield, Manchester, Hull and Liverpool. To assist him in this task Roberts and his immediate successors gave Colin virtually carte blanche to travel the country. This was not always to the liking of his colleagues in the other regions, particularly when they discovered that his car had been upgraded for the purpose from the ubiquitous Ford

Popular to the more up-market Morris Minor – normally reserved exclusively for national officers.

However, the task of recruitment proved particularly intractable in relation to those feudal strongholds of Oxford and Cambridge. As Alan Fisher told the TUC in 1965,

"In the cloistered citadels of our oldest universities – Oxford and Cambridge – the battle for proper trade union recognition has still to be won. I have a vivid recollection of leading a union delegation to meet the Council at Kings College. I half expected to find a body of elderly gentlemen with mutton-chop whiskers, adorned in ruffs and lace. I was, to say the least, somewhat taken aback when a number of them confided to us that they were avowed socialists. And three openly declared their membership of the Fabian Society. It does not say much for the stamina of our intellectual friends that we are today still without proper recognition at Kings College – or any other Cambridge college for that matter".

Colin decided that his first target would be Balliol College, Oxford, with which his old mentor R. H. Tawney was connected, in the belief that such an influential contact might prove decisive. Unfortunately this proved to be a complete misreading of the situation because, when it came to non-academic staff in an Oxford college, the domestic bursar was god and the academic staff had virtually no influence. And the domestic bursar at Balliol at that time just happened to be a former senior manager at The Savoy, with whom Colin had crossed swords previously during a demonstration about working conditions there. It was therefore to be some time before NUPE breached the Balliol defences.

Nonetheless there were useful sources of support to tap into. One organisation happy to offer advice on obtaining an entrée into colleges and universities was the Association of Scientific Workers, who had no reason to fear the rivalry of a union for manual workers but who were presumably pleased to see the expansion of the trade union movement generally in the university sector. In Nottingham he had useful support from Ken Coates, an extra-mural lecturer, many of whose students were funded by the NUM. There were also unexpected sources of help such as the Head Porter of one Oxford college who turned out to be a local organiser for the Communist Party.

Even outside Oxbridge there were pockets of resistance. In Wales, for example, the employers insisted on conducting side meetings in Welsh even in Colin's presence. At Oundle School an official strike was called in opposition to the school's refusal to recognise the union. The widespread press reports of upper middle-class mums breaking picket lines to ensure that their poor deprived sons did not starve was one of the more heart-warming stories associated with NUPE's activities on Colin's patch.

However, elsewhere in the public sector the battle was far less bloody. Head teachers who themselves had joined a union (or "professional association") for their own protection could scarcely justify denying the same benefit to their cleaners and dinner ladies. In fact, Colin soon discovered that the recruitment of dinner ladies was less problematic than the school cleaners. The cleaners were responsible to the school caretaker who, although probably a member of one of the public sector unions himself (and they were usually men), was less keen to see his assistants unionised. Dinner ladies, on the other hand, could more easily be approached direct. In any case, in the immediate post-war years and the 1960s there was growing and overt left-wing sympathy among senior managers in the public sector. Whether this was the residue of the war or the result of more liberal educational philosophies can be argued interminably but it was certainly noted by trade unionists at the time that these recruitment drives often felt like pushing at open doors.

The most important breakthrough was to gain access to staff records, and therefore home addresses, to facilitate postal recruitment. It was also enormously helpful that so many public organisations were prepared to agree to the direct deduction of union subscriptions from wages and salaries. On the face of it this may not appear to have been a wise move on the part of the employers. However, at the same time they were seeking union co-operation in simplifying the payment of wages, using cheques and bank accounts and, in return, it was not difficult to extract this important *quid pro quo* from union officers, even if the members themselves would have preferred to receive their pay in the more traditional coin of the realm. Also, perhaps uniquely then among

NUPE officers, Colin readily agreed to pay to the employer a small percentage of any membership fees collected by direct methods as a contribution to the administrative costs of collecting them. Not only did this 'oil the wheels', it also established a financial relationship that gave the union greater leverage, even if the union hierarchy were not convinced. Later, in the north-west, one of the most reluctant of the large shire authorities to agree to direct approaches to its employees through the payroll was Lancashire County Council. However, the Authority was decentralised into a number of geographical Divisions for the administration of education and the approach adopted by NUPE was a salami tactic, picking the Divisions off separately and then leaving the county headquarters with a *fait accompli*. NUPE officials had to be cunning as well as awkward.

In matters of recruitment in NUPE Colin is acknowledged as having been peerless. Ever the pragmatist and wheeler-dealer, he set new standards for the expansion of membership. He may well, for example, have been the first to use pre-paid envelopes in recruitment – a small investment for a lifetime's membership. As membership forms were returned in response to his recruitment initiatives he used his wife and children at the weekend to process the applications. This exploitation both of his wife and children (whose pocket money was incidentally dependent upon their clerical efforts) and of the opportunities presented by postal recruitment enabled him later in his career to treble the size of his membership in the north-west in 14 years and to boast that, had these members belonged to an independent union, they would almost certainly have qualified him for a seat on the TUC General Council.

Politically Colin found Nottingham far less congenial than Sheffield. While the broad political complexion of the city was not too dissimilar, socially it was very different. The active involvement of the church, the university and the middle classes generally in the working life of Sheffield, and therefore to a large extent in its politics, was markedly different from the situation in Nottingham. This was parochial politics with a strong whiff of graft and corruption, with a tendency to oppose anything remotely progressive. There was also the perennial warfare between city and county to divert energy from any kind of common purpose. And involvement in the union was for many the route into the kind of politics which Colin always found distasteful.

This impression was reinforced for him when the city fathers refused to agree to the deduction of union subscriptions from wages for NUPE members when they had readily agreed to the same arrangements for the rival unions. Colin was not to be put off so easily and was prepared to do whatever was necessary to recruit members surreptitiously, often by visiting roadmen on site. His retaliation to this poor treatment of his union was to advise his members not to vote Labour in the forthcoming municipal elections – an opinion which was to find its way on to the front page of the Nottingham Evening Post. This was by no means the last occasion on which, for the greater good of his members, he was to dissociate himself publicly from the party of which he was a member for the best part of 50 years.

His squeaky clean image which he maintained throughout his career and political life was something he wore with some pride. Never taking payment or expenses for outside activities (except to pay them into the NUPE coffers), refusing any of the perks of public office and openly disapproving of those colleagues (as well as opponents) who fell short of his own high standards did not make him popular in some quarters and especially among NUPE colleagues, whose commitment to the service of the membership he saw as rather less complete than his. "Sea-green incorruptible" is a phrase that might have been coined for him had it not already been done to death in late eighteenth –century France. In fact the only bribe he recalls ever being offered overtly was a quantity of dried sewage for his roses from the manager of the local sewage works in Bradford, who opined that it would "suit his personality extremely well". Even this enticing offer was declined.

Colin's next mission for NUPE was a transfer to the north-east in 1966, again at the Union's request and again without any financial benefit. It was a posting that only lasted two years and this time he took over an existing office with established routines. Initially he found the Geordie accent quite impenetrable and at only his second branch meeting in Northumberland he was completely unable to follow the discussion. So when his opinion was sought he took a gamble by identifying the most intelligent-looking chap in the group and announcing sagely that he agreed with him. Fortunately this seemed to meet with general approval.

He also had the good fortune to be able to explain away his appearance in full stage make-up before a meeting of members in Newcastle. Since a predecessor had been a flamboyant homosexual, it was clear that the working men of Newcastle feared that Colin was cast in the same mould. Luckily for him they seemed to be convinced by his (truthful) explanation that he had come direct from representing their interests in the television studios, where in those days even the hands had to be made up before appearing in front of the cameras.

Although this was to be a short-term appointment, there was nothing of the caretaker in Colin for, in those two years, he doubled NUPE's membership in the north-east from 25,000 to 50,000 and opened about a dozen new branches. This did no harm at all to his growing reputation inside the union, where he was beginning to be seen as a rising star, and every new member represented additional income, thereby stabilising NUPE's finances in the process.

Nor did he experience any resistance from the local authorities in the area. A large proportion of the elected members were ex-miners, members of the Labour Party and wholly sympathetic towards the low-paid. However, the response of competitor unions, such as the GMBU, was more hostile. Andrew Cunningham of the GMBU, later to be embroiled in the Poulson bribery scandal, was instrumental in arranging for him to be offered various places on public bodies to try to bring him under control. On one occasion Arthur Bottomley MP offered to help Colin become a Member of Parliament and on another he was telephoned personally by Richard Marsh, Secretary of State for Transport, to see whether he would allow his name to go forward for membership of the Regional Passenger Transport Authority. Since it is highly unlikely that his name would have come to a minister's personal attention at that stage in his career without some outside intervention, and since it was well known that such recommendations were only made in the north-east with the benefit of Cunningham's patronage, it did not take Colin long to reject both offers.

Tyneside in the mid-sixties was experiencing grinding poverty in the wake of a collapsing ship-building industry and shipyard closures. There was surprisingly little militancy there, possibly as a result of the triumph of Methodism over Marxism, but also there was the heavy hand of the Roman Catholic Church operating almost like a freemasonry in the region. On reflection, Colin now feels that he quite underestimated the Roman Catholic Church's influence on the area's affairs but the experience stood him in good stead for his later role in the north-west.

During his time here he continued to have a national role in recruitment in the university sector. Indeed he was given virtually carte blanche in this field, firstly by Bryn Roberts and subsequently by Sidney Hill and Alan Fisher. In Newcastle he enjoyed considerable success since the Vice-Chancellor not only encouraged his workers to join NUPE, but also became a member himself. This was of course a splendid advertisement for the union but eventually Colin had to ban the Vice-Chancellor from attending branch meetings as his presence inhibited his porters and other university employees from speaking openly. It is also said that his membership of NUPE denied him the knighthood that his post might otherwise have warranted.

Also at this time the young Rodney Bickerstaffe, who was later to become the union's General Secretary, worked under him. Rodney's mother was an active NUPE member in Rotherham and she had ambitions for her son to make a career in the union. So when he graduated from Rutherford College, Newcastle, she wrote to Sidney Hill, the General Secretary, on his behalf. He was given an immediate interview and appointed on the spot; clearly the union had fewer qualms then about the operation of nepotism. Colin, who by now was himself a rising star in the NUPE firmament, particularly in relation to his work in the university sector, was asked to take him under his wing. Bickerstaffe was the first graduate that NUPE had employed and was therefore already something special, although there was no such thing as a fast-track graduate career in the union; reputations and promotion had to be earned the hard way. Indeed, for most recruits it was seen as a distinct advantage that they had gained their school certificate.

The first task which Colin set the new boy was to go out and recruit 200 members from schools in Newcastle as part of a wider campaign. It has to be said that the climate in the north-east was not hostile to this kind of recruitment since the head teachers themselves were heavily unionised and would give every encouragement to their staff to follow their example. However the new officer discharged the task successfully. It was clear to all that the young Bickerstaffe had ambitions that extended beyond a local role and he was quite prepared to move at the union's behest to advance his career. He was soon to find his way to national headquarters in London, via a relatively short stay in Leeds.

There was a time when Colin too had felt that he himself might have a future at the hub of the union, perhaps as the union's National Organiser, where his recruiting skills could have been utilised on a much wider canvas. It is also interesting to speculate how NUPE's stance nationally might have been influenced in the national disputes that ensued if Barnett had been in a more influential position. However, he was unsuccessful in his quest for that post and for him, in any case, the disadvantages of a life in London heavily outweighed any ambitions he may have had in that direction.

Although he may well have been disappointed at the time, he now accepts that being based in the provinces, well away from the steely stare of headquarters, gave him far more scope to speak out on a wide variety of issues over the years. However his ambitions were encouraged, albeit perhaps inadvertently, during his time in Newcastle when Sidney Hill invited him to address all the union's officers nationally at Ruskin College, Oxford on his success in recruiting members. As he was still a relatively junior officer and his own divisional officer was perceived as having been by-passed for this honour, it is not surprising that the accolade was seen by many as premature and resented accordingly.

5. THE NORTH-WEST

The move to Oldham in 1968 at last represented a proper promotion to the senior post of Divisional Officer for the north-west. While NUPE was heavily centralised in its administration and finances, it delegated considerable operational responsibility and freedom to its Divisional Officers and it was at divisional level that many careers were established. For example, the impressive Alan Fisher, who succeeded Sydney Hill as General Secretary (also in 1968), had previously been a dynamic Divisional Officer in the West Midlands. And Colin Barnett lacked nothing in dynamism.

Fisher was a fine public speaker. He was also one of the most effective mob orators of the twentieth century, who was quite comfortable breaking into song at the annual conference to encourage his members to "keep right on to the end of the road!" and to leave a lasting impression on all who heard him. Fisher was the second of Colin Barnett's NUPE heroes. He had joined NUPE straight from secondary school in 1939 as a junior clerk and had worked his way up through the union. He was a powerful advocate for the low paid and for the protection of public services, particularly when he perceived that they were under threat from both the Heath and Thatcher governments. Nor did he pull his punches when Wilson and Callaghan led Labour governments. So the 1970s were to be a period of continued expansion in the union's membership and, in addition, one of increased militancy.

Whereas his other postings in NUPE had been for relatively short periods, it was clear that his appointment as Divisional Officer in 1968 would be of longer duration. Indeed, short of a promotion to the Union's headquarters in London, it might well be the last step in his career – a sobering thought at the early age of 39. His arrival in the north-west coincided with a period in the history of industrial relations in Britain that was fractious and militant. There was a growing view in the country that the proliferation of strikes was causing serious damage to the economy that Harold Wilson's government (1966-70) had worked so hard to restore. The most compelling case was being made by the regularity of unofficial strikes led by "Red Robbo" and his ilk in the West Midlands motor industry, but other industries and the public services were also being affected. It seemed that the union hierarchies were either unable or unwilling to control the excesses of their local officials and shop stewards.

The Labour Government's first reaction was to set up a Royal Commission under Lord Donovan to make recommendations to improve the situation. However, the outcome was far less decisive than ministers had hoped, since Donovan's emphasis was not on action to curb union power but on constructive measures to improve industrial relations. His principal recommendation was for an "Industrial Relations Commission" to examine in detail where the existing system had failed. This seemed to Wilson and to his Secretary of State for Employment, Barbara Castle, to be just too little and far too late. Indeed Castle was quickly coming to the view that sharper weapons were required in the form of penal sanctions against unions that resorted to unofficial industrial action and this proposal became a key feature in the White Paper "In Place of Strife", published in 1968.

When the document was welcomed by the Conservative Opposition and attacked by many Labour MPs as well as the entire trade union movement, it was clear that Castle had a serious battle on her hands. The response of the TUC was to publish its own "Programme for Action". This offered the Government a plan for regulating unofficial strikes but stopped short of legal penalties. When Castle's Bill came before Parliament it soon became apparent that it could not succeed and it had to be abandoned. Across the country this was portrayed as a victory for trade union militancy and proof positive that a Labour Government was unsuited to prosecuting a struggle with trade unions successfully.

In the general election which followed at least one of the reasons for the Conservative victory was a belief that they had the greater political will to deal with the problem and, once elected, they set about the task with a vengeance. In the ensuing post-mortem there was a widely-held belief that the unions had lost the election for Labour and there were many in the Party who felt that they deserved now to reap the Conservative whirlwind.

So the newly-appointed NUPE Divisional Officer had to make his way in a region where industrial militancy was rife, with both of the main parties nationally competing to prove that they had the political muscle to bring the unions to heel.

The new General Secretary, Alan Fisher, was a fine trade union leader who inspired great devotion among his staff. However, his managerial skills were perhaps less well honed. They seemed to consist mainly of letting his dogs off the leash to cause maximum pain both industrially and politically, providing that they made no unauthorised calls on the Union's budget, since his scheme of delegation certainly did not include money. It would be an understatement to say that Colin did not find this operational latitude uncongenial. Indeed he thrived on it and probably pushed its boundaries to the very limit. And if he overstepped the mark from time to time it is highly unlikely that Fisher would have made much of it beyond some general exhortation in fine rhetorical style.

One former colleague described Fisher as "remote", recalling that every encounter with him was conducted in the same way – addressing the other man like a public meeting. It is said that one NUPE officer left the room to answer a call of nature during a telephone conversation with his General Secretary and that, when he returned, Fisher had not even noticed his absence. Colin himself recalls walking along the seafront at Barmouth with Fisher, soon after the latter's retirement to Wales, and discussing a possible role for him with an industrial tribunal. Colin's disability made it difficult for him to keep up with his companion and he soon fell yards behind. However, Fisher was holding forth with great passion and failed completely to notice that for some time he had been speaking only to himself.

Colin Barnett (right) with Alan Fisher

NUPE's North West Division had some problems in 1968. Some of the senior officers were openly resentful that they had not received the promotion to Divisional Officer. Some of them seemed to Colin less than totally dedicated to the union's cause. Indeed one colleague routinely refused to attend evening meetings because it would interfere with his responsibilities at Leigh RLFC, where he was chairman. The new broom decided to sweep some of this dead wood away without standing on too much ceremony – an act which was never likely to gain him great popularity among his new colleagues.

NUPE's membership in the Division in 1968 was 30,000 and recruitment was to be the new boss's top priority; so by 1984 the number had more than trebled to 100,000. This exponential growth was the result of a number of Barnett initiatives referred to earlier; postal recruitment and the deduction of union subscriptions at source, for which he insisted on paying the employer a 5% fee, thereby establishing an enduring business relationship and freeing union officers to spend their time more productively than in collecting money from existing members. This enabled them to concentrate more on the creation of new, often small NUPE branches in the rural areas of the north-west.

Colleagues who worked with Colin in his early years in the north-west still pay tribute to his fearless leadership, his skill as a negotiator and his willingness to engage in battles on as many fronts as were necessary; one even likened him to a nuclear missile. However, they had less regard for his managerial abilities; (or, as one former colleague asked succinctly, 'what management skills?'). Among former colleagues the consensus is that he appeared shy and aloof and many openly admit that they feared his icy criticism. Even senior colleagues found him "difficult" because he seemed to be absolutely certain about everything and brooked no argument whatsoever. While many may have admired him, it seems that none was close to him and he has maintained contact with hardly any former colleagues in retirement. To those he respected and trusted it seemed that his style of delegation was as limitless as the General Secretary's; to others he seemed constantly to be meddling and undermining their more pedestrian efforts. One such officer became so exasperated that he announced that Colin had "done for him" and resorted to ordering a full load of ready-mix concrete to be delivered to the front drive of the Barnett house in Oldham. This character only survived in his job because wiser colleagues intervened and forced him to cancel the order just minutes before it was executed.

Not all of Colin's projects were successful. The NUPE office in Bebbington, Cheshire was the base for five smoking and one non-smoking officers. As a non-smoking, teetotaller himself, Colin was determined to arrive at a negotiated agreement to improve the working conditions of his non-smoking colleague. But, in spite of his best efforts and the exercise of his prodigious negotiating skills, the matter remained unresolved and the non-smoker decamped to the south of England to escape the stench of northern tobacco.

These were not the days of managerial professionalism in the trade unions. The Barnett style may have been seen as "flying by the seat of his pants" but, in fairness, this was no more than the world expected. When incensed at the non-payment of some money by Westmorland County Council he immediately called a press conference and threatened to impound a County Council roadroller. If this was viewed as precipitate and irresponsible posturing, he would no doubt have pointed out that he had taken the precaution first of consulting the solicitor, Roger Pannone about the lawfulness of his plan. And when Pannone pointed out to him that neither of them had driving licences which authorised them to drive road-rollers, he thought nothing of adapting his plan and impounding some typewriters instead. The County Council were embarrassed, the outstanding bill was paid and, perhaps most important of all, NUPE had the best of the publicity.

He was seen as energetic and as having an original and fertile mind but, with no one effectively restraining his campaigns, it is perhaps surprising that none of his escapades really back-fired on him. In part this was because accountability in the 1970s was less well-developed than today. But it was also because his style was in tune with the leadership of the union, which seemed to be growing in confidence by the day. In contrast, the style of the rival public sector unions was excessively hierarchical and conservative. For them, respect for the Bridlington Agreement which regulated (i.e. prevented) the transfer of members between unions was seen as crucial.

NUPE tended to take a rather more relaxed view but for Colin it was merely an encumbrance to be circumvented. At one stage he even dismissed it as a treatise on building sandcastles! One former colleague, who greatly admired Colin's recruiting skills, nevertheless described him as a "complete maverick" and proffered the view that perhaps even the majority of his new members were poached from the other, less dynamic, public-sector unions. This is probably an exaggeration for Colin still characterises his efforts more as "organising the unorganised"; but it is perhaps one of the wonders of trade union history that he was never in his career actually cited before the TUC Disputes Committee. Certainly he did not give the impression of being too fastidious about where he found his next batch of NUPE members.

However, his apparent carelessness for the traditions of trade union organisation is not just to be ascribed to a maverick tendency. For deeply embedded in his approach to his trade union and political life was a streak of unbending principle which his sympathisers found admirable and his detractors characterised at best as sheer awkwardness. This puritanical streak made him extremely difficult to assimilate into any organisation where a certain degree of compromise was a natural and justifiable expectation. One of his former senior colleagues has characterised Colin's approach as that of a battering ram, leading from the front to breach the employers' walls. However, the same colleague added that it was fortunate that he also had staff better suited than himself to "tidying up" afterwards while the Divisional Officer had moved on to a completely fresh battle.

If NUPE was able to accommodate this tendency without too much pain, the same could not be said of the Labour Party, which found him a constant thorn in its side. On moving to Oldham, Colin naturally joined his local Labour Party branch and by 1972 he had been elected to the Borough Council for the Clarksfield ward. Subsequently he represented Hartford ward. However he soon found his fellow-councillors exceedingly insular and was constantly in dispute with them.

Group meetings lasted 3 or 4 hours at a stretch but they seldom seemed to address important policy issues; rather they were concerned with the minutiae of council business and the rewards of public office. When he discovered the range of perks available he was outraged. He challenged in turn the ready supply of cigars and biscuits, the mayor's holiday in Scotland in the civic Rolls Royce and the preferment of councillors' relatives in the council's employment. When Colin's own wife was appointed to a Headship in Oldham there were allegations that he too had joined the "gravy train" but he had taken proper precautions in declaring his interest and when the allegations persisted he consulted Roger Pannone, and duly received an apology. This was to be the beginning of a long association with Pannone and his firm, to whom Colin regularly referred clients with grievances.

His perception was that his fellow Labour councillors were from relatively poor backgrounds and in poorly paid employment and that they were all too easily seduced by the creature comforts that membership of the council bestowed on them. Moreover, council membership gave them a significance that would otherwise have been denied to them and they would not give it up willingly in any circumstances. Consequently greater importance was attached to "sticking together" than to improving the lot of their constituents.

He also disagreed with the rest of the Labour members on a significant number of policy issues as diverse as the management of the Playhouse and the level of council house rents. Initially he expressed his discontent simply by walking out of group meetings out of sheer boredom but he gradually became more and more detached from the group. Threats to suspend or even expel him had no impact because, unlike his colleagues, membership of the council was not such an important feature of his life. Long before his term of office was complete he knew that he would not seek another. He resigned from the Labour group and sat for three months as a "Christian Socialist" before taking the final step and serving out his time as an Independent.

He continued in active membership of the Labour Party for another 20 years but he was always to be found on the far-left and usually in confrontation with the leadership. While he would probably argue that the Party he had joined in 1945 had gradually deserted him over the years and failed to live up to its high principles, it is also perhaps true that his was a resignation letter just waiting to be signed. Indeed some of his friends doubt that he could remain a member of any group for long without resigning on a point of principle. So his survival in the Labour Party for some 50 years clearly indicates a level of emotional commitment, and perhaps affection, that even a lifetime of disappointment could not easily destroy.

He now believes that the Labour Party was probably never sufficiently left-wing for him and that the Communist Party would probably have provided a more congenial home for his leanings. Indeed, had he been born a decade later, there is perhaps a stronger chance that he would have taken that route.   Yet, from the outside at least, it seems somewhat curious that one of nature's rebels should expect to find a natural billet in one of the least tolerant and inclusive political movements of the last hundred years.

6. RUSSIA

The other difficulty with Communism, of course, is that throughout Colin's working life it was inextricably linked with the Eastern Bloc and the confrontations of the Cold War. Nevertheless a number of people in Britain belonged to the British version of the Communist Party, among them some leading Christians, writers, intellectuals and artists. Indeed, as we have seen, some of Colin's earliest mentors in the Church of England were committed communists and proud to declare it. During the Second World War the Russians had been seen as vital allies in the fight with Nazism and there was considerable admiration for the bravery and suffering of the Red Army and the Soviet people. However, for most British people the descent of the Iron Curtain and the Cold War stand-off meant that adherence to the Communist Party justified suspicions of disloyalty for the next forty years or so.

For left-wingers and pacifists such as Colin this was a serious cause for concern. His instinctive sympathy for a regime built, however tenuously, on socialist principles led him from the outset to entertain political sympathy for the soviets, while his pacifism, which first emerged in his membership of the Peace with China movement, was offended by the armed build-up and threatening postures of the Cold War. As a youth he had been involved with the Anglo-Soviet Youth Friendship Alliance with Billy Marshall. He had also taken a leading part in Sheffield in the opposition to nuclear testing and had become a member of the Campaign for Nuclear Disarmament.

For Colin and people like him in the peace movement there was a strong public suspicion that they were at best the naïve and idealistic dupes of communist infiltrators, whose agenda had more to do with serving Russian interests than with preventing nuclear war; at worst they were seen as fifth-columnists. When they joined CND marches and addressed their rallies they were generally vilified for their willingness to make common cause with such characters and were depicted in the media as anything other than peacemakers. Whether or not they were naïve, they were certainly aware of the hostile attitude to their involvement and yet they still continued to court the publicity which only added to their denigration. Certainly no one could level the charge of cowardice at them. However, there is no doubt that these organisations were infiltrated in the way the popular press described and there were real dangers in such associations. The names of Burgess, Philby and Maclean had not been forgotten, while that of Blunt was still to emerge.

One of Colin's strongly held views was that the cause of peace would be enhanced if only the ordinary people of the west and the east could have greater contact with each other. He felt, for example, that British and Russian parents had a shared fear of nuclear war and a common interest in promoting a better future for their children, irrespective of the posturing of their political leaders. Standards of living might vary from one economy to another but individual aspirations paid no heed to national boundaries. He believed too that personal contact between individuals would reduce the suspicion and convince them that neither really intended the annihilation of the other.

In furtherance of these aspirations Colin joined the Manchester - Leningrad Friendship Society and was part of a 90-strong delegation from Manchester to Leningrad. Since he was seen there as an influential and prominent trade unionist he was treated extremely well and special efforts were made to enable him to see what he wanted. He visited people's homes and met for the first time Helen Petrova and a number of prominent Leningrad intellectuals with whom he was to maintain contact over many years.

Helen herself was the first visiting professor from Russia to be attached to a British university. This was at Bradford University where Harold Wilson was Chancellor. It seems likely that such a development was largely at his instigation or at least to have involved his personal influence. For Helen herself the placement may have been something of a mixed blessing since, on her return to Leningrad, her colleagues remarked on the alarming deterioration in her English accent! She also confused her academic colleagues in Bradford by insisting on ostentatiously reading the News of the World over Sunday lunch.

Many further visits to Russia followed, mainly to Leningrad but also to other parts of the country. On one such excursion to Yalta they discovered that Leonid Brezhnev was also visiting the town and decided to write him the following letter, which was drafted in the Hotel Yalta:-

"Dear Friend

We the undersigned, being a party of British visitors to the Soviet Union, associated with the Manchester-Leningrad Friendship Society, wish to express our concern for world peace and harmony. We wish to state our belief that all nations should seek positively to work hard for mutual understanding and avoid a return to the Cold War.

We wish to place on record our respect for the achievements of the Soviet People, our appreciation of the friendship that has been shown to us whilst we have been in the Soviet Union and our recognition of the enormous sacrifices made by the USSR in the war against the Fascist regimes.

On our return to Britain we will inform our friends of your continuing desire for peace and friendship."

Yours sincerely

Colin Barnett (and 68 other signatories)"

The letter was subsequently published in Britain in Soviet Weekly (9 September 1978).

The excitement of being able to see Soviet society at close quarters and the affection which Colin and his colleagues obviously felt for the Russian people emerges clearly from the text. The location itself may well have added to the mood, associated as it was with the historic meeting between Roosevelt, Churchill and Stalin. Whether it was a wise thing to do to write so fulsomely to Brezhnev personally about his "continuing desire for peace and friendship" is more doubtful. Certainly there were few back home in Britain who would have seen the Soviet General Secretary in such a light, even if they shared Colin's "respect" for the Russian people, and many might well have seen the letter as ill-judged and sycophantic. The charge of political naïveté was clearly not without some foundation. Indeed Colin still maintains that they just did not care how the initiative would go down at home, even though they would be likely to be seen as apologists for a tyrannical regime. Yet it seems not to have occurred to them that they also had the opportunity to draw attention to the abuses of the Soviet regime and the many limitations on human rights to be found in Russia.

However, outside of the politics, Colin was responsible for giving many of his British friends and acquaintances the opportunity to see Russian life at first hand. These were not just trade union and left-wing associates but included a wide range of professionals and academics, keen to compare the two systems of government in relation to their own disciplines and fields of interest. A couple of British MPs even took advantage of the opportunity although at that time they considered it prudent not to advertise the fact and travelled incognito.

One notable participant was General Sir Hugh Beach, then the Warden of St George's House, Windsor and certainly no sympathiser with the Soviets. He was obliged to obtain permission from both the War Office and the Foreign Office to join the visit and was convinced that he would be specially targeted for seduction or that he would be compromised in some way, even though Colin pointed out that this was unlikely as his wife was accompanying him. In fact, as far as anyone is aware, no such attempts were made although whether that was because of a failure in Soviet intelligence or because he was in the company of their distinguished visitor from NUPE is not known. However, his presence in the party did result in a higher level of security and an increase in the number of body searches. Interestingly, Beach subsequently started the "Edinburgh Conversations" with representatives of the Russian military and was a member of the Security Commission under the Thatcher Government. What part his trip to Leningrad played in these developments is not known.

Colin also recalls that, on their departure from Heathrow, Beach was somewhat dishevelled in appearance. So, when Colin's mother-in-law arrived to see the party off, she mistook the General for a porter and offered him a tip. In spite of his appearance, Beach was clearly a true gentleman since he accepted the offering with good grace rather than embarrass a lady by telling her his proper identity. When the party arrived in Leningrad they were immediately whisked off to see a school play, which involved three separate casts, all speaking impeccable English. Beach was so impressed by this that he was certain that the youngsters had been imported from Moscow especially for the occasion.

As the visits became more frequent it became more acceptable for "respectable" people to take part. Colin and his family became regular visitors and stayed in the homes of their Russian friends. A standard programme was developed and circulated widely (even if it was usually scrapped on arrival in Leningrad!). Soon the Directors of Education in two boroughs in Greater Manchester permitted the programme of visits to be circulated to the staffs in their schools and subsequently a number of schools throughout the north-west were engaged in staff and pupil exchanges.

Leningrad continued to be his main point of contact with the Soviet Union. With some 27 universities it regarded itself as the academic and intellectual capital of Russia and very much despised the provincial upstart Moscow that had become the capital of the USSR. It was also the centre of the Soviet defence industry. The people they met there were extremely curious about their British visitors but had no high regard for their educational standards, particularly when they discovered that Colin could not speak knowledgeably about the subjunctive mood of verbs. They, on the other hand, were educated (to the horror of the socialists among their visitors) in a selective system which was not immune to manipulation by those with influence.

The Russians also displayed some oddly conflicting attitudes. For example they seemed to take a high moral stance over the allegations of homosexuality that emerged in the Jeremy Thorpe trial yet they were avid "Monopoly" players (when Colin managed to bring in illicit pocket sets) and asked their western guests to bring with them the latest Barbie dolls which, for the first time, had been given breasts. The visitors had to be warned about attractive Intourist guides who were actually KGB agents, who made official reports on all the foreign guests, and against importing bibles into the country. Nonetheless, when Colin checked whether it would be possible to import a copy of Salman Rushdie's "Satanic Verses" for Helen Petrova, he was told there would be no problem. In the event by far the bigger worry was that the suitcase which contained it was mislaid and, when it reappeared in Leningrad, it transpired that it had found its way there via Karachi!

Colin himself was something of an enigma to his Russian hosts. In a country which is heavily dependent on alcohol and where persistent efforts are made to entertain visitors by endless toasts and eventual inebriation the presence of this total abstainer was a serious challenge. But he made close friendships with his hosts and became a frequent and welcome visitor. He was never refused permission to visit anywhere although the authorities kept a tight control on the people he was permitted to speak to. Certainly there was no chance of speaking to dissidents although, when one visitor with a theological bent asked to meet with an Imam, a Rabbi and an Archbishop, he was taken aback to find that all three turned up at the same meeting.

One thing that puzzled Colin was why, whenever he visited Helen Petrova, he was never able to meet her son, a physicist who held three professorships. This went on for over 10 years and it was only subsequently that he learned that the man worked in atomic physics and his work was clearly felt to be too sensitive for him to come into contact with foreigners. As the effects of *perestroika* and *glasnost* came to be felt many of these earlier restrictions were lifted and eventually Colin and his family were able to meet the professor. When Colin's infant but precocious daughter Amy asked him what atomic physics was, the professor replied kindly that he would explain when she was older. This did not satisfy Amy who said that would be no good because he might be dead by then!

Another man, the husband of an eminent biographer of Lenin, was always away fishing when Colin visited. Since the man often asked for new fishing lines to be brought from England, Colin accepted that the explanation for his absence was quite plausible. Only subsequently did he discover that he had had to make himself scarce as he was the Admiral in charge of the Soviet nuclear submarine fleet. To have met with foreigners would have run for him the risk of being denounced to the authorities.

Visitors were always impressed at the quality of English spoken in Leningrad, usually with upper-class accents; at the daily news sheets pasted to the walls, which appeared to give versions of the news which were similar to those encountered in the west; and at the knowledge and interest taken by their hosts in the British Royal Family – again a surprise for the ardent republicans among them.

Their Russian hosts were apparently always pleased to meet British guests; from the Russian teachers who swam around an entire bay at Yalta, because they had heard English being spoken, to the Leningrad doctor who stood successfully as an MP citing in his election address his acquaintance with British people as a reason for supporting him.

Colin once found himself invited to give a eulogy at the funeral of a friend's husband. This was a very traditional religious ceremony which also involved kissing the corpse and he recalls that all went well apart from the fact that his oration may have lost some of its impact because the interpreter was in floods of tears. The continuing role of a thriving church in the officially atheist USSR was another surprise for visitors and, for a man of religious leanings like Colin, perhaps somewhat puzzling. When he is pressed today to explain how a religious man can justify his long-term support for an atheist ideology he still struggles. He argues, somewhat unconvincingly, that Russian communism was only atheistic because of the corrupt nature of the Russian Orthodox church a century ago and that communism in Britain would not necessarily be the same. But it is interesting that he is still prepared to suspend his normally acute critical faculties in favour of the old Soviet Union when he would never have made an equivalent concession at home.

In fact, whatever the initial motives for his visits to Russia, by the time we met in the mid-1980s it was apparent that his prime concern was for cultural exchange. Not only were British acquaintances encouraged to join one of his trips, they were also involved with Russians who were helped to visit Britain. Russian doctors, teachers, administrators and politicians all found their way to the Barnett home in Merseyside, some to visit and others to live and work for extended periods. They even included a younger Vladimir Putin before his career brought him to national and international prominence. It was fascinating to hear their impressions of Britain. Some found the streets of Merseyside considerably less safe than Leningrad; they marvelled at the high costs of public transport; and compared the British telephone system unfavourably with that at home, where calls were free within the city. It may however have been a surprise to them that there was a telephone directory freely available whereas, at home, the telephone numbers of other people were shrouded in secrecy.

Colin and his family had a Russian au pair for over two years. In that time she saved virtually every penny she earned both as an au pair and by delivering the local free newspaper, so that she could take home with her £2000. In contrast, those Russian visitors who had to save money in order to support themselves on a visit to Britain seldom came with more than a few hundred pounds and were dependent on the generosity of the Barnetts and their friends.

Since Colin was by now a regular visitor to Russia he once complained that he knew more about the Russian military than their NATO equivalent. So, when the opportunity arose to visit NATO headquarters with a north-west TUC delegation, he leapt at it. The invitation was actually issued while Colin was attending a CND meeting and he wondered subsequently at the unlikely circumstances. Whether there was an underlying motive involving Special Branch can only be a matter of conjecture. Whatever the explanation, he clearly felt the need to be less circumspect in his exchanges at NATO Headquarters than in the Soviet Union. When he met the then Secretary General, Joseph Luns told his visitors how upset he was that the influence of the left wing in Europe had denied him access to the new neutron bomb. Colin's response was that he therefore felt fully vindicated in his opposition and Luns stopped the interview at once. It seems that the NATO hierarchy were as unused as their Soviet counterparts to encountering people who disagreed with them.

It seems clear too that Colin's approach to the two sides was rather less than even-handed; he applied far more critical standards to his expectations of his own government than to those of the Soviets. Yet he would be the first to concede that the openness of the NATO hierarchy with a group of trade unionists far exceeded that of his Russian hosts, however congenial their company. He also seems to accept the irony of the position of the Peace Movement. For, however sincere their objectives, it is now generally recognised that the fall of the Berlin Wall and the end of the Cold War owed more to the unbending policies of the American and British governments in the 1980s than to the influence of CND. The further irony, of course, is that the current proliferation of nuclear weapons to a wider range of states has produced far greater instability than the Cold War ever spawned and that the Peace Movement seems powerless to make any significant impact.

However, on a broader front, Colin's involvement in exchanges with Leningrad certainly bore fruit in terms of professional, educational and cultural exchanges for the north-west region and, as we shall see later, in the unusual turn taken in his retirement.

7. THE DAY JOB

Ask an officer in any trade union about the purpose of his job and he will doubtless tell you that it is to advance his members' interests and to protect them from overweaning employers; to be "articulate on behalf of the inarticulate". The quest for ever more favourable conditions of service and better rates of pay is eternal. Delve a little deeper and he will tell you about the day-to-day business of consultative committees and the individual casework involved in disciplinary and grievance hearings that are the bread and butter of his working life.

In a public sector union such as NUPE, which existed to serve the interests of the lower-paid and manual workers, there is never any shortage of this kind of casework. The immediate supervisors of these workers are often scarcely more skilled or able than the people they manage and there are always clashes of interest or personality to be resolved. Moreover, the public services are highly labour-intensive and involve regular personal contact with the more vulnerable groups in society such as sick patients, young children and people with learning difficulties, and their carers.

The scope for conflict is wide and yet, for the most part industrial relations in the public sector are relatively peaceful and civilised compared with some industrial settings. The usual fare is a charge of misconduct of a fairly mundane nature or an allegation of unfair treatment or bullying from an over-zealous supervisor. Much of it is resolved informally at a local level without recourse to the full-time staff of the union. But if the issues at stake are more serious, leading to possible loss of employment, or if the problem remains intractable, a more experienced full-time officer may well become engaged in the dispute, providing a more articulate and experienced advocate for the worker than would otherwise be available.

What is also apparent, however, is that many public sector managers are often found wanting when confronted by the more forensic and combative approach of the full-time officer, who has no reason to pull his punches in defence of the member. And by all accounts Colin Barnett was not an adversary to be taken lightly. He prepared quite meticulously. If there had been any procedural irregularities, however minor, he would be bound to find them, since it was apparent that he knew an organisation's disciplinary or grievance procedure better than those who had written it. Managers seemed to freeze like rabbits in his headlights and he had a sharp but fluent tongue and the tenacity to match, which made him a difficult opponent; the word "formidable" featured regularly in interviews with old adversaries.

He believed that his members deserved his very best

advocacy, irrespective of innocence or guilt, and it was not an infrequent outcome of disciplinary cases involving Colin that patently guilty union members survived in their jobs because he had managed to demonstrate errors in the management case, whether procedural or factual. One such case involved an alcoholic hospital porter, who had been sacked for being drunk on duty. Colin took the man's appeal and won it because, in spite of the overwhelming evidence, the prosecution had been prepared so badly and without due regard for the procedures that the man was re-instated and received 6 months' back pay. Since his second wife Hilary, who was by now herself a NHS manager, was on maternity leave, he had asked if she could attend the hearing as an observer. When the meeting was over and the outcome known, she was visibly shocked at the incompetence of her managerial colleagues and simply could not understand how Colin had "got away with it".

As his reputation spread, it can have done nothing but good for his recruitment figures and the fact that Barnett was riding into town often caused otherwise confident managers to review their cases with some urgency and to make extra efforts to arrive at amicable settlements to avoid having to be cross-examined by the NUPE Divisional Officer.

Some of his tactics were also unpredictable and unorthodox. On one occasion he asked for an adjournment of a disciplinary hearing to enable him to take part in a live interview on a BBC Radio programme on a completely unconnected issue. Remarkably, the tribunal agreed, sat quietly while he was interviewed and then politely applauded his performance before resuming the hearing. On another occasion he wrong-footed a hospital secretary in Stockport who had boasted that he would negotiate with Colin at "any place" and "any time" by demanding a meeting at 6 am on a Sunday morning. To his credit the hospital secretary kept the appointment but, when he offered Colin an early morning drink, NUPE's teetotaller was horrified to see thirty or forty empty whisky bottles in the cupboard. Nor did traditional managers know how to handle a little round pacifist with a disability who persistently challenged them to fist fights. The bizarre challenge was never taken up, of course, although no-one who knew Colin would doubt his commitment to the threat.

His resourcefulness was legendary, particularly in the field of recruitment. In Ashton-under-Lyne he once recruited 700 members in a month. In an area with a strong Catholic influence he always carried with him a copy of the Papal Encyclical which recommended Catholics to join trade unions and never hesitated to use it. However, his relationships with the Roman Catholic Church were always uneasy. He was surprised to see the level of influence which the Catholic Church exercised in politics in the region. Often this influence was used to the very great benefit of the community by Archbishop Derek Worlock in his close association with Bishop David Sheppard. However, Colin now feels that there was also a more malign influence in evidence in some of the local councils and in trade union affairs, which he failed to identify fully at the time.

But there was also a darker side to Colin, since not all of his methods were kosher. At one stage senior NHS managers in Merseyside became quite paranoid at his apparent ability to anticipate their every move in a dispute. What they did not know was that an ex-burglar known to Colin was breaking into their safe at night and copying papers that might be useful to the union. If the Barnett conscience was troubled by the illegality of these actions, there was precious little evidence of it. The priceless explanation he offers is that such underhand tactics would have been unnecessary if only the other side had operated with more honesty and openness.

Colin's tenure in the north-west had begun in 1968 in strident opposition to a Labour government's proposals to reform industrial relations and the strength of the trade union movement's reaction had been a major factor in Wilson's defeat in 1970. In the same way the "Winter of Discontent" of 1978 sealed the fate of Wilson's successor, James Callaghan, in 1979. The economic recession which confronted the Callaghan government is well documented. Rising inflation and unemployment and the need to resort to a $3,900 million loan from the IMF led the Chancellor of the Exchequer, Denis Healey, to try to persuade the unions to accept a series of caps on wage increases. Initially his strategy had the reluctant support of the TUC, which in May 1976 agreed to limit average wage increases to 4.5%.

By early 1978, the economic crisis seemed to be easing and it seemed likely that the Prime Minister would use the opportunity to call a General Election since he was being sustained in power only with the co-operation of the Liberal party in the "Lib-Lab Pact". When that collapsed, only the support of the Scottish and Welsh Nationalists, in the expectation of substantial constitutional devolution, was propping him up. In spite of many difficulties in Parliament, the Government's 'Scotland Bill' finally passed into law in late 1978 with a referendum planned for 1979. So, although an early election seemed prudent in the light of the improved economic indicators, Callaghan resolved to soldier on into 1979.

This proved to be a bad mistake as the mood in the country was turning strongly against the Government's pay restraint policy. Vauxhall Motors employees gained a rise of 8.5%; the Ford workers achieved 17%. Strikes by lorry drivers and tanker drivers, supported by widespread secondary picketing, resulted in a pay increase of 14% which broke the Government's cap of 5% so significantly that it appeared that the floodgates must open. And with such large pay increases being negotiated in the private sector the public sector unions, including NUPE, were concerned that their members should not fall behind. But against a background of rising criticism from the Conservative Opposition, led stridently by Margaret Thatcher, that the Government was caving in to the unions, Callaghan resolved to impose sanctions on firms that broke the 5% limit and to make a stand against the pay demands of the public sector employees, thereby painting himself into a corner.

The industrial trouble that ensued became known as the

"Winter of Discontent" because of the high level of disruption caused in the public services. At one point 1.5 million public sector workers were on strike. The demand from NUPE and the other unions had been for a 15% rise – well above the Government's maximum target of 5% - and in spite of informal signals from the unions that an offer of 6% might well be sufficient for them to call a halt to the disruption, Callaghan quite incomprehensibly refused to budge, even though moderate trade unionists warned him that they would be unable to deliver a settlement on his terms.

The disruption to national life was serious and in the health service in particular the unions trod a very fine line, for any real threat to the health of patients could have lost them the support they appeared to enjoy from the public at large. GMBU gravediggers in Liverpool went on unofficial strike and Liverpool City Council had to hire a factory in Speke to store the coffins that were piling up; the Medical Officer for Health in Liverpool even speculated that burial at sea might have to be considered. Photographs appeared daily in the tabloid press of rubbish piling up in London parks as a result of a strike of refuse collectors. In fact NUPE's campaign was conducted extremely skilfully at national level, promising that no patient would be put at risk and that emergency cases would be handled in the normal way, even though the workers would not be paid.

In the end Callaghan had to accept a settlement of 9% plus £1 a week to bring an end to the chaos created by public sector strikes but by then his economic policy was seen to be in complete chaos and, when the election was held in May 1979 after the loss of a vote of confidence in the Commons, a Conservative Government was returned with an overall majority of 43.

Subsequently former Labour ministers blamed the public sector unions for their fall from power. Barbara Castle, in her book "Fighting all the Way", was more circumspect, attributing the defeat to a variety of factors, but in private she was adamant that this was the case and opined that none had played a bigger part in their defeat than Colin Barnett. At the time neither Colin nor any of the other union leaders were at all repentant as they felt they owed it to the lower paid to protect their wages at a time of high inflation but, if they had known then what plagues the new Tory Government would visit upon them, it is doubtful whether they would have been quite so uncompromising in their demands or so militant in their actions.

However, during the 1979 election campaign Colin did encourage his members to vote Labour, even if his endorsement of the party's record was less than enthusiastic. He described Margaret Thatcher as a "short-tempered and short-sighted" woman. He warned that she would pursue a policy of confrontation with the unions, cut public expenditure and increase unemployment.

It was in the field of health principally that Colin flexed his muscles and those of NUPE during his time as Divisional Officer. After 1979 the combination of

Thatcherite politics at national level, the fractured state of society in Merseyside, and the determination of NUPE nationally and regionally to accept these challenges with relish, all served to create a period of serious industrial unrest.

The height of this struggle came in 1982 in a dispute in the NHS that lasted 8 months. The background to this dispute was what was perceived generally in the country as a determination on the part of the Government to take on and defeat both the trade union movement and the entrenched attitudes of the public services. This included a constant stream of proposals to put various parts of public services out to competitive tender, which undermined the security of employment of thousands of low-paid workers.

But the main thrust of government policy was to reduce the cost of the public sector and this required a much tighter control on public sector pay. So in response to a trade union pay claim of 12% the Government offered a mere 4%. Neither side was in the mood for compromise. A national ballot conducted by NUPE rejected the offer by a thumping majority of 191,000 to 1,200 and even the traditionally moderate Royal College of Nursing rejected it by a majority of two to one. In total, some 13 separate unions were involved in the health service and the level of unity they displayed was remarkable, given their previous history. The TUC Health Services Committee called for a three-day stoppage and, in September, a rally in London was attended by 120,000 marchers, with smaller rallies involving other unions throughout the country producing attendances totalling perhaps another 100,000.

The experience gained by the unions in 1978 in the "Winter of Discontent" was now put to good use. More than 800,000 working days were lost in the NHS in those 8 months, yet the high level of public support for the health workers never seemed to waver, which made it more uncomfortable for the Government to remain intransigent. Public opinion polls showed that a large majority of the adult population felt that the NHS gave good value for money and provided a good service. However, this level of public sympathy also made it impossible for the unions to recommend the outright stoppage, that would perhaps have defeated the Government, for fear of alienating public opinion. It was therefore inevitable that a compromise would be reached in the end.

However, in the mean time, there was considerable work to be done by NUPE officials such as Colin Barnett. Their approach was to inflict major industrial damage without putting lives at risk and therefore a *modus vivendi* had to be found with local managers which allowed emergency treatment to carry on uninterrupted. With good will on all sides perhaps the approach could have worked successfully but, given the history of industrial relations and the entrenched attitudes of both sides of the dispute in Merseyside, it was always likely to be tested to the limit. Doctors and managers were clearly trying to bend the agreement to treat even non-emergency cases and shop stewards, constantly on the look-out for potential breaches were no doubt more officious than either their leaders or the management would have wished.

Newspapers were full of stories about doctors having to obtain the consent of porters before patients could be treated and feelings ran high. The trade union response was also to try to use the media to full advantage and Colin was a past master at this, taking up to three or four hours a day to brief the press and to respond to questions. And although his message was stark, he had the oral fluency and cultured speaking voice well-fitted to presenting his case in the most reasonable light. Even when corpses were piling up in Liverpool through the closure of mortuaries by the action of another union, such was the continuing level of public support and solidarity with other unions that Colin never felt the need to point out that it was the GMBU and not NUPE that had taken this apparently mean-spirited action. Or perhaps it was something to do with the fact that the mortuary attendants in Manchester were behaving in much the same way and that they were NUPE members?

Certainly the NUPE hierarchy was unapologetic. When a cabinet minister tackled the Union's leaders about these affronts to the "dignity of the dead" Rodney Bickerstaffe retaliated by demanding to know what the Government proposed to do to enhance the "dignity of the living". During this period it was rumoured that Bickerstaffe would be offered a peerage but that he would accept it only if he could use the title of "Lord Bugger of Bugger-all".

In what became known colloquially as the "Dirty Jobs" strike (because of the menial or distasteful nature of the employment of many of those involved) Colin used his energies to involve as many of his members as possible and to derive maximum publicity from it. He saw it as an opportunity to engage even his most passive members in militant action. Uniformed nurses sat down in Deansgate in Manchester and, when confronted by policemen, sought to hold their hands in a gesture of friendship.

Another stunt was the recruitment of two nude models as NUPE members. In a blaze of publicity Colin announced to the press their recruitment and the establishment of a separate branch for them and emphasised that they would be wearing membership stickers rather than badges with pins in the interests of health and safety. The press even went to the trouble of hiring ladders to look in through the windows of the college at which they were employed in order to try to obtain photographs. It is doubtful that anyone took the stunt too seriously but it served to keep the union in the nation's minds and to demonstrate that even hardliners had a sense of humour.

Colin used his regular lectures at the Manchester Business School to win support there and he even marched in to occupy a television news studio in the middle of a live broadcast to prosecute the cause. As a result of all these carefully choreographed gestures and the courting of the regional media, the strike had more public support in the region than at the outset, in spite of the considerable inconvenience and distress that it brought to vulnerable individuals.

There were also major local disputes, particularly in Liverpool where in 1976, through the unreliability of his own Area Officer, Colin had become personally embroiled in a long-running battle with what he perceived as incompetent management. A more charitable view might be that managers locally had just been saddled by central government with completely unrealistic timescales for the opening of The Royal Liverpool Hospital, a major new hospital formed from the amalgamation of a number of smaller hospitals. Whatever the explanation the dispute locally concerned such detailed issues as staffing levels, work rotas, bonus schemes, work study exercises and fire precautions. However, another major problem for Colin was the militancy of his members (whom he describes as having been in "cloud cuckoo land") and the need to formulate demands that were sufficiently ambitious to secure the support of the membership and yet flexible enough to be acceptable to the management; no easy task.

On one occasion during the dispute he arrived early for a meeting of the "Operational Services Group" with senior health service managers in Liverpool to discuss changes in shift rotas for ancillary workers. When he asked where the meeting was to be held, the unsuspecting receptionist showed him into a room where it was apparent that the management side were about to hold a pre-meeting to agree on their tactics. Seeing that the only table in the room had a tablecloth that reached all the way to the floor, Colin, setting aside his disability for the moment, crawled under it and stayed there for the duration of the meeting, listening intently to the other side's tactics being agreed. As soon as the pre-meeting finished, and to the astonishment of the assembled management team, Colin came from under the table and thanked them graciously for the insight they had kindly given him.

This particular anecdote has entered into the folklore of the NHS in Liverpool and is still recounted with awe by those involved (and many who were not) some thirty years later. It also did much at the time to boost Colin's reputation as a foe to be treated with extreme caution. Indeed one personnel manager in the health service in Liverpool preferred to lock himself in his office when Colin was on the premises rather than have to speak to him. Another manager seemed quite content to vacate his office whenever Colin requisitioned it. Such tales resulted in him enjoying far more latitude than he was entitled to expect.

On one occasion he even organised an occupation of the Regional offices at Gateway House in Manchester and ejected the senior staff. Unfortunately the same building also housed staff of the Canadian consulate and the occupation caused a minor diplomatic incident when some NUPE members helped themselves to some consulate writing paper.

He also discovered that the NHS Regional General Manager was himself a member of NUPE when he complained to head office about the occupation. It seems that senior staff could keep their membership confidential by by-passing the regional and branch structure. When the police were called to evict the demonstrators the inspector announced that his daughter was a NUPE member and that he supported their cause. He therefore refused to evict them providing that they did not cause any damage.

NUPE occupy the Regional Health Authority HQ

In the event a Committee of Inquiry was set up under the chairmanship of Professor Dyson to review the problems and to arrive at a settlement of the dispute. But even here Colin managed to pull a flanker by getting the management side to accept as their own representatives on the committee the Bishop of Middleton, whom Colin knew to be sympathetic to the Union's cause, and Bob

Fryer, a socialist academic, who subsequently wrote the history of NUPE and wore his NUPE badge to its first meeting. These were of course in addition to the representatives of the union side. The subsequent Dyson Report certainly criticised NUPE (and its Divisional Officer personally) for exploiting an already difficult situation but, perhaps not surprisingly given the committee's constitution, their most virulent criticism was reserved for the inadequacies of management.

In the aftermath of the dispute, as attempts were made to improve industrial relations in the Liverpool Hospitals, the management, under pressure from the Ministry, strove hard to persuade the Union to accept legally binding agreements. Seeing his chance, Colin said that he would accept such agreements, providing that they included a stipulation that there should be no compulsory redundancies for 10 years. So keen were they to pin him down in this way that, amid enthusiastic self-congratulation, they accepted his condition without demur; and they lived to pay the price throughout the next decade as various restructurings cried out for the flexibility that compulsory redundancies might have given them.

Subsequently, the Liverpool Echo published the following detailed and thoughtful article on the dispute:-

Guerrilla Warfare and the Hospital Workers: We're not out to Sabotage

When NUPE boss Colin Barnett says that the NHS is one

of the brighter jewels in the Labour movement's crown, more than a few eyebrows are likely to be raised. For the statement of belief in the NHS seems to contradict the militancy of his membership's activities in Liverpool's health service……. . But those who try to make NUPE's 47 year-old North-West officer an Aunt Sally for their claims that his union is out to sabotage the City's health care will find him a powerful adversary. With all the practised skill of a full-time trade union official of 20 years standing his defence is typically tough, self-confident and hard-hitting…….

"I see myself as a trade union officer working in one of the most difficult industrial relations situations in any hospital authority in Britain. I believe in management by justification and many of the actions of management in Liverpool have been totally unjustified. This has led to the type of industrial relations they deserve", he says.

"One would hope that highly skilled management expertise would be a top priority in the NHS to settle the disputes as quickly as possible in the interests of the patient. But we seem to be moving toward argument of force rather than force of argument."

He admits he is highly politically motivated in his involvement in the health service and has no time for the argument that politics have no place in a hospital. He describes himself as an unrepentant Socialist and attacks society's lack of a social philosophy…………

He believes a national heath service should be more

107

concerned with preventive rather than curative medicine,
staffed by well qualified people who believe that good
medicine is the right of everyone, irrespective of class,
with adequate facilities being available on the basis of
assessed need.....

"I prefer professionals. I know exactly how far I can go.
If each side is aware of the limitations and the rules and
professional status of both are accepted, you will have
much better industrial relations. ...."

NUPE with its army of 3,000 ancillary staff members
from hospitals throughout the Liverpool area is indeed a
force to be reckoned with. But one, Colin affirms, which
is prepared to sit around the negotiating table. The
ability to negotiate hangs, as far as he is concerned, on a
more open system of management and a far more willing
recognition of and co-operation with unions.

"I am not out to sabotage the service and other parts of
Merseyside have effective industrial relations. There is a
tremendous challenge for management in Liverpool to
create an equally effective atmosphere of negotiation",
he concludes.

Whatever the validity of his views, the article gives a fine
insight into the man who held them and the determination
and skill with which he argued them. Certainly no one
could doubt his courage.

Only three years later, in 1979, he also led a dispute not
with the megalithic NHS but with Leonard Cheshire

Homes – a target which enjoyed massive public sympathy but which, according to Colin was "run by middle-class do-gooders with little or no idea of industrial relations". The Sun's report of the dispute was written in typically robust fashion:-

"A few weeks ago, during the picketing of a Leonard Cheshire home for the disabled, Mr Barnett threatened to make the name of Leonard Cheshire 'stink throughout the trade union movement'. Group Captain Leonard Cheshire is, of course, the war hero who won his VC fighting to keep this country free so that people like Mr Barnett can have their say".

This dispute did not begin ambitiously. All the Union were seeking were rates of pay and conditions of service for ancillary staff that were equivalent to those in the NHS. However, the Leonard Cheshire Trustees simply refused to negotiate or to recognise the union in spite of the fact that many of their employees were members; hence the reference to "middle class do-gooders with little or no idea of industrial relations". Such a target was not likely to win NUPE much public sympathy but they persevered with the strike and picketed the home in question and eventually the Trustees, with considerable encouragement from the Anglican Bishop of Liverpool, David Sheppard, agreed to recognise the Union and to accept the case for better rates of pay and conditions of service.

Throughout his service in NUPE Colin was always to be seen wearing his NUPE tie and badge, leaving even the casual observer in no doubt as to his role and his whole-hearted commitment to the cause, even at times of great unpopularity. Other unions found this single-mindedness a sign of his unwillingness to co-operate fraternally. The Regional Secretary of the rival health service union COHSE said:

"Mr Barnett is more interested in winning new members. We are for people who are sick. For example in the catering department we feel we should, even if we go on strike, at least ensure the patients receive one hot meal a day. He does not care for such considerations".

That was nothing less than the truth; Colin's message was far more uncompromising (and his syntax far less garbled too). Any appearance in the media was to him an opportunity to advertise his Union and to attract new members. Everyone with whom he came into contact recognised his unwavering determination and anyone who tried to distract him with small talk or conversation about extraneous matters failed miserably.

However there was one extraneous matter that did reinforce his prominence in the national press. During the latter phase of the Callaghan government it became apparent that a General Election might have to be called at any time. Prospective parliamentary candidates were therefore selected well before the usual stage in the life of a parliament and among these was a Manchester dental tutor Dr Hilary Hodge, who was selected for Wallasey, a marginal seat held for the Conservatives by Linda Chalker with a majority of 1,800. Hilary was an outspoken and left-wing candidate and, together with the newly selected David Blunkett, she was offered sponsorship by NUPE in the forthcoming election. As the Divisional Officer for NUPE Colin was therefore asked to offer her whatever assistance she required in fighting the seat.

It soon became apparent that Colin and Hilary shared a common political creed and over the next few years they became closer personally too. The 1979 election produced a substantial swing to the Tories so she did not win the Wallasey seat but her political career began to blossom locally. In 1981 she was elected to Merseyside County Council and sat on the Merseyside Police Committee, where she and a number of her colleagues had cause to challenge the then Chief Constable, Kenneth Oxford, over a wide variety of issues. Such was the level of distrust between them that the Committee began to tape-record the proceedings in order to be in a stronger position to challenge the minutes of meetings, which they felt were not a true record.

As her relationship with Colin developed there were the inevitable claims that he was manipulating her in her attacks on the Chief Constable, particularly after the Daily Mail reporter spotted him passing her a note during a particularly contentious meeting. The note was actually about their arrangements for tea but the press could not let that detail get in the way of a good conspiracy story. So the headline the following morning read,

"TUC Chief runs Police Authority through partner".

Not surprisingly Hilary was more incensed than Colin by the report. "If you think I'm a puppet or a front woman, I can assure you I'm not", she said to the local press. "I take great exception to the suggestion that I'm not able to take my own political decisions". She was also annoyed at the suggestion in the press that the ripe language she often used had been learned at home from her (older) partner. In fact Colin seldom swears in spite of Hilary's influence.

Colin was divorced from his first wife, Margaret, in 1982 and he and Hilary set up home together in Prescot. Prescot forms part of the borough of St Helens but after they had moved in they discovered that for parliamentary purposes they were constituents of the former Prime Minister, Harold Wilson, in Huyton. Conspiracy theorists were certain that this was a conscious decision and that their aim was to discomfort or even to unseat Wilson, whereas the truth is that they had simply not done their homework properly.

There was the usual tabloid scandal about their relationship. The Daily Mail in particular assigned a reporter to stalk them in order to publish the usual exposé. So when they married in September 1982 the only photographer present was from the same newspaper and, in one of those ironies with which politics is littered, when Colin asked the paper to let him have copies for the family album, they duly obliged! Subsequently in 1984, when Colin retired, the Daily Mail reminded its readers

"In September 1982 his marriage to dental officer Dr

Hilary Hodge, 32, made news. They attended a strike rally, a council meeting and their wedding at St Helens Register Office, all in the space of four hours".

A bigger surprise would have been if they had taken the full day off.

8. THE REGIONAL TUC

Interesting and demanding though it was, Colin Barnett was never the sort of man to be content simply with his "day job". His commitment to a socialist agenda drove him to pursue it wherever the opportunity arose, particularly if he could thereby enhance the reputation of NUPE. One such opportunity arose when there was a vacancy for the post of Regional Secretary of the TUC in 1975. The vacancy arose when the previous Secretary resigned in the aftermath of a controversy about the costs of a cultural festival in the region – something of a financial scandal. As we have seen, the post of secretary was one with which Colin had often become familiar. There was never a shortage in left-wing politics of people volunteering for positions of prominence but he had realised very early in his career that far fewer were eager to take on the actual daily work involved in the position of secretary; and in the case of the Regional TUC the role also brought considerable power and influence, providing unlimited media opportunities and *carte blanche* to comment on any issue of the day on behalf of 2 million workers in the region.

In those days the Regional Secretary's post was part-time and, before Colin could take it on, he had to persuade

Alan Fisher, the then General Secretary, that holding such a position would be to NUPE's advantage in the region, raising both its visibility and prestige. It seems that Fisher was not entirely convinced. He therefore allowed Colin to take the post, in addition to his NUPE duties, for only one year in the first instance. Since he went on to hold it until 1984 it is perhaps fair to assume that he demonstrated to Fisher's satisfaction that he was capable of carrying out both jobs. Or perhaps Fisher took comfort in the fact that Colin's success in recruitment had by then resulted in NUPE's regional membership rising to 100,000, with a proportional increase in full-time staff. So the NUPE membership in the North West was hardly likely to be neglected as a result of its workaholic Divisional Officer taking on yet another responsibility. In fact Fisher, who in other respects was regarded as somewhat tight with money, agreed that NUPE would stand in full the administrative costs of the secretariat throughout Colin's tenure of the post. This came also to include the expense of a weekly information service to the Regional Executive in order to ensure their support for all Colin's initiatives.

While NUPE's remit was to represent lower-paid public service employees, the TUC represented the interests of all trade unions in both the public and private sectors, although observers at the time felt that the thrust of Colin's efforts was unsurprisingly in the public sector. One local private sector employer who fought battles with the printing unions in Merseyside on a daily basis described the TUC in the region as no more than a "loose confederation" of interests, which scarcely impacted on his working life at all. Nevertheless the Daily Mail did remark (unfavourably) on Colin's leadership of a march through Warrington in protest against the Messenger Group proprietor Eddie Shah in his dispute with the National Graphical Association; and his strong interest in raising the profile of the unemployed clearly crossed the public/private divide. The same local employer also thought it sufficiently remarkable to comment that Colin was "not corrupt"!

Since many of the other unions in membership of the TUC had never seen eye to eye with NUPE, particularly in relation to championing the unemployed, the job of representing their collective views on a daily basis and squaring them with NUPE policies cannot have been easy. Nor was the TUC national hierarchy entirely comfortable with Colin's appointment. In fact Len Murray, the relatively moderate General Secretary of the TUC at the time, went out of his way to visit Colin in order to test out his views, since he had a reputation for holding communist sympathies. Murray was therefore quite taken aback when Colin (truthfully) asserted that he was a "Christian Socialist" and seems not to have explored too fully how Colin's version of Christian Socialism differed from his own. However the meeting went well, to the extent that Murray sent Colin tickets for the Cup Final the following year. Since Colin had not the slightest interest in football and on principle never accepted gratuities or favours of any kind, he donated them to a soccer enthusiast in the NUPE office. For Colin it was quite sufficient to have made a favourable impact on the TUC General Secretary and thereby to have cemented his position in the Region.

He interpreted his remit with the TUC very broadly indeed. As Divisional Officer for NUPE he had to confine his public pronouncements to the business and policies of his union, but his TUC role imposed no such limitations. He submerged the press with news releases and spent hours every day speaking to any part of the media that would listen to his views on current issues. Alan Fisher was even surprised early one Sunday morning to hear Colin launching a theological defence of the "closed shop" on a Radio 4 religious programme. Much as he might now find the connotations of the term distasteful, Colin was surely one of the early and highly effective exponents of the art of "spin". And, since he held his position not through the patronage of the General Council but had been elected to it by the regional membership, he was also able to retain a degree of independence in his role that his appointed successors never again enjoyed.

His high-profile position also involved him much more actively in the political life of the region. Having moved into Harold Wilson's constituency, albeit inadvertently, he and Hilary became thorns in the ex-prime minister's flesh. As he neared the end of his parliamentary career the last thing he would have welcomed was two articulate, middle-class left-wingers taking an active part in constituency affairs. They were constantly proposing resolutions with which their moderate MP was uncomfortable and, although they were usually defeated, there was speculation that either or both of them were positioning themselves to succeed him. This reached a climax in the following report from the Liverpool Daily Post in February 1981:-

Keep to the Loyal Centre, Wilson urges Huyton.

Former Prime Minister Sir Harold Wilson, who has announced that he will not seek re-election as Huyton's MP, immediately fired the first salvo in the battle to find his successor.

Speaking in Liverpool yesterday, Sir Harold said the Huyton constituents would go for a candidate who belonged to the "loyal centre" of the Labour Party.

And he rules out NUPE and North-West TUC leader Colin Barnett as a possible successor.

"The Huyton members showed recently they were not interested in Colin Barnett or others of his political ideas when he failed to get a majority vote on a resolution criticising views I expressed on the television," he said.

.... Last night NUPE leader Colin Barnett said he would not be standing as a candidate for the Huyton seat.

"I have never had any political ambitions whatsoever but I have considerable ambition in seeking to influence the election of a new candidate," he said.

'I have no idea who that candidate will be but my support

will go to a good, left-wing socialist concerned with the
transformation of society rather than the preservation of
the existing order.

Others thought that they knew exactly whose candidacy
Colin would eventually support but Hilary also took the
opportunity to deny her interest in the seat.

Apart from politics, Colin had always taken a keen interest in broadcasting. He has an educated voice and is
extremely articulate, setting him apart from the
stereotypical view of the average trade union activist.
Even in his time in Newcastle he took part in a religious
phone-in each Sunday. It was in one of these that he was
accused of owing more to "St Marx than to St Matthew".
In the north-west he progressed to become a regular
contributor to regional television programmes,
particularly on Granada Television, where he perceived
that many of the people responsible for current affairs
programmes held political views not dissimilar from his
own. Indeed there appears to have been quite a body of
sympathy there for the Socialist Workers Party.

One of Granada's programming initiatives was "This is
Your Right", introduced by the former Liberal MP, Dr
Michael Winstanley, which explained to viewers their
legal rights on a whole variety of issues. Colin became a
regular contributor and for 19 years was "employment
adviser" to the programme, giving advice to viewers on
employment law. Here he gained a reputation for
explaining complex matters with clarity and objectivity
so that, although his responsibilities there precluded him

from overtly recruiting members, it is perhaps not surprising that NUPE's recruitment of new members always increased significantly in the days following one of these broadcasts. For anyone wary of his firebrand public image would certainly have been reassured by his professional approach on the screen.

He also appeared on Granada's "You the Jury" espousing the cause of the closed shop. The debate was chaired by the former Labour MP for Lincoln, Dick Taverne QC, and Colin caused some sweaty palms right at the beginning of this live programme by challenging the neutrality of the Chairman on the grounds that he was a member of the Bar, one of the most influential of all closed shops. The Conservative MP, Nicholas Winterton, led for the opposition and he too was challenged as a former officer in the Grenadier Guards – another organisation Colin depicted as a closed shop. He had clearly done his homework in "Who's Who", much to the annoyance of the blustering Winterton. He also rigged the debate by packing the audience with NUPE members, who had been instructed to vote against the closed shop at the beginning of the debate only to change their views at the end. Since the programme was subsequently broadcast more than once, the "repeat" fees also helped NUPE's coffers.

If his reputation regionally was as a smooth and tireless media operator, as well as a formidable debater, his standing with the national press was hardly high. Throughout this period his outspoken views were often an embarrassment to those newspapers trying desperately to demonstrate that the Labour Party was still an electable party, contrary to the evidence piling up to the contrary. On the other hand, the press that had thrown their weight behind the Thatcher government scarcely let slip any opportunity to represent him as a danger to the nation.

For example, in 1979 he had written on behalf of NUPE to Labour MPs in the region, warning them that they risked losing the support of NUPE members if they did not back the union's campaign for workers on low pay.

The spin put on this statement of the blindingly obvious by The Sun was as follows:-

Colin Who?

Mr Colin Barnett, NUPE's chief official in the North West, is not very well at the moment. He is suffering from an acute and painful case of swollen ego.

He has written to Labour MPs in the area warning them that NUPE will support only election candidates who back the Union's campaign on low pay. In other words MPs must be puppets who dance to NUPE's tune.
....

Fortunately Mr Barnett's latest attempt at bully-boy tactics has misfired badly. Mr George Rodgers, Chairman of the North West Group of Labour MPs, said on BBC Radio yesterday that they all strongly resented Mr Barnett's interference and that he had been very unwise to write to them in such a tone.

Splendid!

The more people who rumble this self-opinionated pip-squeak the better.

Some people would have been wounded by these insults but for Colin even this kind of publicity was no more than par for the course and he rationalised that it kept the voice of the left to the fore. Neither battered nor bowed he simply rejoined the media battle reinvigorated.

On one occasion he found himself invited to a Directors' lunch at the Guardian to discuss the economy of the pre-war Weimar Republic, only to discover that they had intended to invite not Colin Barnett but Joel Barnett, the former Labour cabinet minister. Needless to say, he had researched the issue thoroughly and he seems to have managed to hold his own in the lunchtime debate. He recalls that the occasion was actually most convivial and that, since it was on the same day that a peerage was announced for Harold Wilson's controversial assistant Marcia Williams, there was a certain amount of ribald discussion involving the late Brian Redhead about the title she might take.

Throughout his working life he never sought refuge in an ex-directory telephone number or set any store by the protection of his personal privacy. Such were his feelings on the matter that, when one of his NUPE full-time officers decided to defy his Divisional Officer and go ex-directory, Colin took the matter all the way to Alan Fisher himself. Needless to say Fisher agreed with Barnett.

His activities were seen by the Thatcher government as sufficiently threatening for his telephone to be tapped. Normally an individual whose calls were being intercepted might not be aware of it but, since the engineers working on his line were also loyal trade unionists, they knocked on his door one evening to warn him. Thereafter, every time Colin answered his telephone, he began by announcing his support for a pay rise for MI5. The eccentric Chief Constable of Greater Manchester, James Anderton, is said to have referred to him as a "reptile" that should be "crushed under policemen's boots".

His participation in public demonstrations and marches was not therefore risk-free. His campaigns in support of the mineworkers and other industrial causes also gave ample evidence of the threats posed to dissidents by an increasingly politicised police force. On one occasion during the miners' strike he was travelling to the Midlands for training as a marriage guidance counsellor (another spare time interest) when his car was intercepted by the police and he was told not to travel any further. His protestations that his journey had nothing to do with the industrial dispute fell on deaf ears, although the Marriage Guidance Council did subsequently receive a decent apology from the police for this treatment.

On another occasion he was called from his bed in the

early hours because a carpet shop next door to the NUPE offices had been destroyed by fire. Appearing on the scene wearing a pullover over his pyjamas he was annoyed to find a policeman taking his photograph. When he protested he was assured that it was part of the normal routine of the investigation into a suspicious fire since the arsonist sometimes returned to the crime scene to see the extent of the damage. Colin was assured that his photograph would be destroyed but the sting in the tail was that they assured him that the constabulary had enough pictures of him already.

His activities were not limited to industrial issues. He was also a founder member of the North West Peace Council, an ad-hoc body established to promote peace and friendship with Eastern Europe, which also involved fund-raising and visits to eastern-bloc countries at the height of the Cold War. His involvement in such causes never put him in any severe danger but it did lead to incidents of low-level harassment, in which police officers became implicated, although officially the police line was that he was not considered important enough to trouble Special Branch.

However, he also owed his personal safety to police intervention on more than one occasion. His involvement with the North West Peace Council and the North West Committee against Racism made him as many enemies on the far-right as his trade union activities. He worked actively to counter the growing influence of the National Front and on one occasion even managed to print and distribute over one million leaflets attacking them. These were paid for entirely by donations from Jewish businesses in the region.

This activity led to his life being threatened by Column 88, the neo-Nazi group. When he reported the threat to the local police, the superintendent advised him to take it very seriously indeed and provided him with police protection, masquerading as road-menders outside his house. On another occasion a plain clothes police inspector rescued him from a threatening National Front audience at a public meeting he had called to attack racism and smuggled him through underground passages to the car park. Clearly there were individual officers in the Greater Manchester Police who detested the thugs of the far-right even more than they disapproved of Colin's brand of left-wing socialism.

The irony of these personal risks, taken in support of causes about which he felt passionately, is that Colin could never be confident that the views he held would have been supported by rank-and-file NUPE members or the wider trade union movement in the region. For, although they could be violently left-wing on matters of pay and employment, their attitudes on social issues often did not differ far from those of the racists he had the courage to attack; such are the complexities of working-class politics. He did, however, have the safety net of the steady support of the Trades Councils who were also able to nominate representatives on the committee of the Regional TUC.

If there was a single, key achievement which marked

Colin's tenure at the TUC it was the shift that he managed to bring about in the TUC's attitude to the unemployed. In 1975, when he assumed the Secretary's role, the attitude of trade unions generally to the scourge of unemployment was one of stunning lack of interest. Of course TUC leaders spoke sympathetically about the plight of those without jobs but they could not be persuaded to take any concrete action that might actually help the situation, believing that they owed their primary duty to their own members; after all, the unemployed paid no subscriptions.

Over the next ten years things changed dramatically. Firstly there was a massive increase in the unemployment figures which could not be ignored. But of more significance in mobilising the unions was the fact that these trends could be attributed directly to the policies of a government they disliked intensely. Nationally NUPE used its influence, increasingly strengthened by its growing membership, to press the case of the unemployed while in the north-west Colin Barnett and his supporters worked in more practical ways to mobilise opinion. All of these (and other) efforts helped to shame the TUC into a less supine position.

9. THE MANPOWER SERVICES COMMISSION

Quite early in his career in the north-west Colin became aware of attempts to set up an enterprise agency in St Helens to sponsor the development of new small businesses. The story of this pioneering initiative is expertly told by Ian Hamilton Fazey in his book "The Pathfinder", which charts the efforts of the pioneer Bill Humphrey to create Britain's first agency of this kind with the support of Pilkingtons the glassmakers. He and his sponsors reacted to economic decline in the area by trying to establish an agency which would help embryonic small businesses to obtain finance and impartial advice and thereby create new jobs to replace the more traditional routes into employment.

During the 1980s such agencies sprang up all over the country until they became an integral feature of the economic landscape through "Business in the Community", but this first such initiative experienced numerous obstacles and setbacks. One of the early problems Humphrey experienced was the unwillingness of the trade union movement to involve itself in the project. We have already seen the traditional reluctance of the conservatively-minded TUC to champion the cause of the unemployed, preferring instead to limit their efforts to the more direct support for their (working) members. Later, as the Thatcher government tightened the screws on the economy and presided over a massive increase in unemployment, the unions were forced to re-think their positions, but in the late-1970s they had not really begun to contemplate such a conversion. Moreover, Humphrey's embryonic enterprise agency seemed to have more to do with support for bosses than for the workers of Britain. So any trade unionist who co-operated with him was likely to be seen as some kind of maverick.

Hamilton Fazey writes:-

"Humphrey believed he should always try to get the most senior person he could reach when trying to sell his ideas and this proved fortuitously important when he set out to obtain trades union support. Instead of going to see the St Helens Trades Council, with its strong anti- Pilkington element, he decided it would be better to approach the highest-placed local TUC official he could find. This proved to be Colin Barnett, secretary of the TUC's North West Regional Council. In Labour Party terms, Barnett, a Christian socialist, is regarded by most observers as well to the left. ....But when Humphrey called on him........ Barnett not only liked the idea Humphrey put before him but immediately offered his good offices to help. He even hinted that if asked he would be willing to serve on the Trust's board. Humphrey was tempted to take up the offer but had already set his mind on restricting board membership to people who lived in St

Helens or who worked there or who had other connections that committed them at first hand to the community. Ironically Barnett was later to become a St Helens resident but by then ill-health had forced him into early retirement from his TUC post. In retrospect, it is probably unfortunate that Barnett was not able to join the board, for his left-wing credentials would have been in good order as far as many Socialist fundamentalists were concerned. Yet as a senior TUC officer he had long experience of the "moderate" trade unionists' role of always, finally, opting for the best deal for the vast majority of the membership, even if that meant that there had to be an element of compromise."

That the St Helens Enterprise Agency subsequently went on to blaze a trail nationally for similar initiatives is greatly to Humphrey's credit and shows his great tenacity. And although Colin Barnett in the event did not become actively involved in the project his response to Humphrey's approach says much for his open-mindedness in the context of unemployment and heralds one of the other major roles that he was to play in the north-west.

This proposition was even more intriguing than Humphrey's and it came out of the blue in 1978, when Dewi Rees, the Regional Director of the Manpower Services Commission approached Colin about becoming Chairman of the Area Board for Greater Manchester and Lancashire.

The MSC was a quango created by the Heath

Government's Employment and Training Act 1973 in response to the general perception of a training crisis in Britain and it survived until it was transformed into the Training Commission in 1988. The principle behind the Act was that for Britain to regain its position as a major industrial power there needed to be a sea-change in national attitudes to enterprise, work and the creation of wealth. The MSC was to play a major part in this transformation through the medium of training. It consisted of representatives of industry, trade unions and "other interests", including education and local authorities and it reported to the Secretary of State for Employment. The Commission's remit was principally in the field of manpower planning and was intended to link training and job creation, particularly in the area of skill shortages. But from the outset there was disagreement about the extent of its role; the Labour Opposition wanted it to have a much greater say in the overall planning of the labour market than the Government would allow, while the TUC wanted it to act principally as a job creation agency.

Then in the 1974 General Election a Labour government was returned. Its election manifesto had promised to turn the MSC into "a powerful body responsible for the development and execution of a comprehensive manpower policy". However, as unemployment started to increase following the oil crisis of 1973, the attention of the Commission was diverted from this grand design to the task of creating short-term job training schemes for young people and, in spite of budget reductions elsewhere in the public sector, its funding and staffing were increased massively to tackle this problem.

So the Area Manpower Board which Colin Barnett was to chair for five years was essentially the local arm of a quango which had huge discretion in the allocation of public funds to create short-term training and employment. Why, even under a Labour Government, the chairmanship should have been offered to a maverick like Colin remains a mystery. To this day he has no idea who recommended him for the post. However, it appears that the Regional Director, Dewi Rees, had considerable freedom in such a selection and Rees himself had something of the maverick tendency. Although a civil servant, he had a significant trade union background and an instinctive sympathy for the unemployed. On the other hand his image was not generally seen as squeaky clean since his personal property deals while in office caused questions to be asked in Parliament. He did, however, have a reputation for getting things done and it may well be that he saw in Colin a man with similar energy levels. His appointment was not popular with the employers' side but Rees stuck to his guns, as he continued to do for some time even after the election of the Thatcher Government in 1979, since Colin remained in post until 1983.

Although the strategic remit of the MSC was a hot topic of political debate nationally, for Colin the task in the region was relatively straightforward. Here was an opportunity to do something practical to provide jobs for the unemployed and to use government money to do it. For a man with his agenda this was akin to winning the lottery, especially as he and his Board had over £1,000,000 to spend every week.

Bishop David Sheppard had been appointed only the year before to the equivalent post for the adjacent area of Merseyside and, when Colin ceased to be chairman of his board, he served as an ordinary member of Sheppard's for a further three years, until 1986. Sheppard throws useful light on the role in his autobiography "Steps Along Hope Street";

"I chaired the board, with its monthly meetings for eight years. Much of the MSC's training has been criticised; it was generally judged by the yardstick of whether it led to a "real job". But that depended on the availability of "real work" in that particular area.................In areas that seemed like industrial deserts, the Youth Opportunities Programme (YOP) often provided training that changed a youngster's attitude to service for the good of the community. Supervisors were often grandfatherly figures who had been made redundant, but passed on positive approaches to time-keeping, reliability and care for needy people."

The issues in the neighbouring board would not have been very different and no doubt the solutions were also similar. But what marked out Colin's approach to the job in addition was the often divergent ways in which he used the massive funds available to him.

Firstly a number of research posts were established both in NUPE and the North West TUC to strengthen their campaigning roles. Indeed, it appears that MSC funds were used to finance the TUC regional office in its entirety. Clearly this was not what the funding was intended for but nor was it precluded from the rubric according to which Area Boards were required to operate. Moreover these were certainly demanding and interesting posts, albeit on a temporary basis, attractive to bright young graduates. If anyone perceived any conflict of interest for the Chairman in creating these positions, very little was made of it. Rees warned Colin that he was sailing close to the wind on occasions but no action was taken to stop him, even on the part of the employers' representatives who served on the Board and who might have been expected to put up a struggle. The benefits to the trade unions in the region of having a bright and active research role was immense and may well have been one of Colin's most enduring achievements.

Another area close to home which felt the benefits of this largesse was the NHS. Colin's new wife, Hilary, had by now been appointed as a District Dental Officer in Mersey Region. She had a strong interest in preventative dental work and was taking on an ever more active role in health promotion. The combination of two fertile and flexible minds produced proposals on a large scale to utilise MSC funds for health promotion work, initially in the field of dentistry but then increasingly on a broader scale. Their first initiative was to involve ten unemployed youngsters on the Youth Opportunities Programme in producing puppet shows. This led to the appointment of unemployed teachers to write dental health programmes which Hilary evaluated for use in schools. There followed a Women's Health bus and support workers for carers. As these initiatives mushroomed it is estimated that upwards of £1 million of the Area Board's annual budget was being channelled into health promotion.

Again the work was of great value in an area where general standards of health were not high and again it was from among a large field of bright and imaginative young graduates that appointments were made. This time, though, there were objections, not from political or industrial opponents but from vested professional interests in the NHS. Dentists in the region took exception to non-dentists becoming involved in their work and some even began a campaign with the General Dental Council to have Hilary struck off. However, the quality of the work being undertaken became recognised nationally in the light of the stringent evaluation being undertaken. Their example was followed in a number of health authorities in the Midlands and the schemes won awards from the Health Service Journal. Even the British Medical Journal came out in support. On one occasion, when she was asked at a conference how she had managed to obtain trade union approval for her schemes, Hilary confided to the audience that she had had to make the supreme sacrifice!

It would be possible to see in these initiatives a major conflict of interest, which in the formalities of a local authority, for example, would have had to be declared and the Chairman debarred from voting or speaking. But the Area Boards were run on much looser lines with the emphasis on speed of action rather than bureaucratic niceties. In any case, it is also possible to see them as a rare case of truly "joined-up" thinking between MSC, trade unions and a major public service. However, they were also taking place under a Conservative Government determined to reduce public expenditure, particularly in areas of operation seen as peripheral to the essential work. It is not surprising therefore that ministers saw Colin's approach to the role as less than acceptable and began to consider how he might be replaced by someone more in tune with Government policies. He was even approached privately to see if he would stand down voluntarily in return for the award of a CBE. However, his response was that he wouldn't consider resigning for anything less than a seat in the House of Lords, a price that unsurprisingly proved to be unacceptable.

Eventually in 1983, some four years after the election of a Conservative Government, his appointment was not renewed and he was replaced as Chairman, receiving no honour at all. However, he did go on to serve as an ordinary member of the Merseyside District Manpower Board until 1986.

10. THE PEOPLES MARCH FOR JOBS

If you were to ask Colin about his greatest individual achievement he would probably refer to the People's March for Jobs in 1981, an event which quite uniquely concentrated the nation's mind on the plight of the unemployed. In the 1979 General Election the Conservatives had ousted the Labour Government with a powerful advertising campaign in the press and at cinemas highlighting the rising level of unemployment which then stood at well over 1,250,000; their graphic depictions of dole queues and the slogan "Labour isn't working" had a devastating effect.

However, the economic policies of the new government served only to increase the number of unemployed even further. With British industry in recession, the first year of the Conservative government saw the figure rise by 836,000 and by the end of 1981 the national total was over 3 million. This figure also has to be seen against the broader background of substantial reductions in public expenditure. Among the new measures introduced were reductions in real terms in many welfare benefits and steep increases in council house rents. The overall effects of these policies were felt particularly keenly in the declining manufacturing areas of the north of England.

The new Government also introduced measures to curb the influence of the trade unions and their power to organise "secondary" picketing, whereby workers in one sector could take industrial action to support striking employees in another. In addition, that traditional stronghold of trade unionism, the public sector, was being assailed on all fronts by a government that seemed determined to transfer as much public sector activity as possible into the private sector through "compulsory competitive tendering". So, while the trade union movement generally may have had deep sympathy for the rising number of unemployed, it had its own pressing problems to address without contemplating also a campaign on their behalf.

Nor did public opinion appear particularly outraged. Regular polls seemed to confirm that, having elected a new government with radically different economic and industrial policies from its predecessor, the electorate accepted that this was a "price worth paying". So the challenge for Colin Barnett and his ilk was to try to influence public opinion nationally.

One of the regions most severely affected by rising, long-term unemployment was the north-west. Merseyside in particular gained the attention of the country through the TV drama series "The Boys from the Black Stuff" and one of its leading characters Yosser Hughes, whose constant demand was to "giz a job". The mood in the area was one of despair and many have argued that the situation was perhaps pre-revolutionary with the danger that the disaffected would drift into the arms of hard left groups such as Militant and the Socialist Workers Party.

In early 1981 there were riots in a number of English cities and it was generally accepted that they were largely racially motivated in Bristol and Brixton. As a result, a commission of enquiry was established under Lord Scarman in April but, before he could report his findings, further riots broke out in the Toxteth area of Liverpool. Since this was predominantly a black area of the city it was tempting to see these events in the same light, particularly when the catalyst for the trouble on 3 July was the arrest of a twenty-year old black youth, Leroy Cooper, in Granby Street. There ensued a weekend of rioting, paving slabs were thrown and supermarkets, banks and other businesses were firebombed. One rioter was killed by a police Land Rover and a few others injured. Over 500 rioters were arrested and some 468 policemen injured; 70 buildings had to be demolished.

The Chief Constable, Kenneth Oxford, said that it was the work of "thieves and vagabonds" who needed no excuse for their lawlessness but local community leaders knew differently and Scarman subsequently confirmed their views in his report. The riots were particularly aimed at the Merseyside police, who had developed a bad reputation for their heavy-handed approach, including beatings, and excessive use of the powers of "stop and search", especially in relation to black youths; the context of the riots was poor educational opportunities, bad housing and chronic unemployment. While the black community in Liverpool no doubt suffered the effects of these social factors more than their white counterparts, this violent reaction was not limited by racial factors and the white residents of Toxteth were equally to the fore in their attacks on the police.

Colin's partner, Hilary, was a Labour member of the Merseyside Police Authority and, together with the Chair, Lady Margaret Simey, another prominent Labour politician, had long been a critic of Oxford and his management of the force. So when the riots broke out both Colin and Hilary broke off from entertaining visitors to attend the scene of the violence. They were shocked to see relatively young children looting from shops that had been damaged and carrying their booty away in taxis, which are of course a far more regular feature of working-class life in Liverpool than in virtually any other city in the country.

The day after the riots Colin hosted a delegation from the TUC General Council and took them to visit the scene. In the midst of the damage and desolation they were struck by the pristine appearance of a completely undamaged Rolls Royce. They quickly discovered that it belonged to the local drug dealer. In the days following the trouble they also hosted meetings in their home involving potential peacemakers such as Archbishop Worlock and Bishop Sheppard and, when subsequently Michael Heseltine was allocated special ministerial responsibility for Merseyside, they worked hard to explain the area's problems to him and accompanied him on visits to introduce him to local people.

Even before the riots began the strong feeling grew that something had to be done to draw attention to the despair that was building up in areas of high unemployment. Colin by now was the elected Regional Secretary of the TUC in the north-west. It is worth stressing that he was elected to this position and not appointed by the TUC nationally so that on this, among many issues, he was able to plough a furrow more independent of national policy than the TUC General Council would have wished.

The initiative for a "Peoples March for Jobs" was not Colin's but was proposed by two Communist members of the Regional Executive. Their inspiration was the Jarrow Marchers of 1936, who had made such an impression on the national psyche through their dignity amidst genuine despair. They produced a detailed plan and a suggested route map for a march from Liverpool to London which was adopted with enthusiasm by the Regional Executive.

The TUC General Council wanted nothing to do with it and did all they could to prevent it taking place but the Regional Executive stuck to its guns and Colin took on the role of Treasurer. He also wrote to the General Council deploring their attitude and telling them that they would lose a golden opportunity to assume the leadership of the movement of unemployed people. In spite of a series of acrimonious telephone conversations, the General Council were unmoved by this argument but the

West Midlands and South East Regions of the TUC gave their support and played a full part in the organisation of the march.

The official leaflet for the Peoples March outlined the situation thus:-

"Unemployment is now a massive problem facing Britain. There are already over 2,500,000 officially registered as unemployed. The real figure is much higher. And the total is rising fast. Each minute one more person is being made redundant. By the end of the year the total will be over 3,000,000. This is a national scandal.

Unemployment is a waste of resources. It means people able and willing to work are denied work. It means the collapse of industries and the desolation of regions. It means industrial decay, not economic expansion. It is also very, very expensive. This year we will pay out almost £1.5 billion in benefit for the unemployed.

Unemployment is a human tragedy. Hundreds of thousands of young people leave school with no prospect of a job or future. Women who have fought for the right to work are forced back into the home. Millions who do have work now live in fear for their jobs. And those out of work now face the prospect of many months, sometimes years, without work. The result can only be misery, desperation, demoralisation and bitterness. Unemployment undermines society.

People must act now. Speak out before it is too late. Say no to unemployment. Millions need the homes, hospitals, schools, goods and services that the unemployed could produce. Demand a return to full employment."

The Peoples March was to set off from the Pier Head, Liverpool, on 1st May and to arrive in London on 29th May, 1981. Its route would take the marchers through the following towns and cities:-

Widnes
Warrington
Salford
Manchester
Stockport
Macclesfield
Congleton
Stoke on Trent
Stafford
Cannock
Wolverhampton
Walsall
West Bromwich
Birmingham
Nuneaton
Coventry
Rugby
Northampton
Bedford
Letchworth
Luton
Hemel Hempstead

Watford
Wembley.

Even before the march began it attracted much sympathy in the region. Representatives of all the churches in Greater Manchester issued a press statement urging church members to think about the needs of the unemployed. They stopped short of supporting the demand for a return to full employment, which they regarded as unrealistic, but concluded:-

"We join in sending our good wishes to all those who will be marching ......and to all engaged in peaceful and constructive ways of drawing attention to those problems, including those associated with the March for Jobs".

Their counterparts in Merseyside took much the same line but also appointed representatives to be in touch with the organisers should overnight shelter be needed in church halls within their area. They concluded:-

"Together we pray for the safety of the marchers, that they may be kept from involvement in violence, and that their efforts may serve to focus attention on the importance of their cause."

The Archbishop and Bishop of Liverpool also took part in an ecumenical service in Liverpool Parish Church on the morning of May 1st as the Marchers prepared to leave. If the references of church leaders to possible violent situations now appear unduly pessimistic it is important to recognise that the Marchers were departing only days after the Bristol and Brixton riots and two months before those in Toxteth. As the situation was so combustible in many urban areas it was clearly vital that the March should remain peaceful and law-abiding, if only for the reputation of the unemployed.

It was never expected that all who set off from Liverpool would walk all the way to London. Indeed, some of the Liverpudlians turned back before they reached the boundaries of Merseyside. However, some 300 set off from the Pier Head and a smaller group started in Huddersfield, to join up with the main group later in Northampton. A third contingent walked from Llanelli. As the march progressed, many others joined it, some for the rest of the route and others for varying distances. For the final leg of the journey into London, the police estimated that numbers had grown to some 40,000.

Because of his growing incapacity, Colin was able to walk with the marchers only for the first few miles; for the rest he had to resort to transport. Indeed for one week of the journey he was in Russia, following its progress, which was very fully reported, in the Leningrad press.

If the intention had been to capture the public imagination the march was a huge success. All the national newspapers gave it good coverage and, with the not unexpected exception of the Daily Mail, they all reported on it positively. Perhaps most surprisingly Louis Herren, the Editor of The Times, travelled the full distance with the Marchers, wearing out two pairs of boots in the process.

Louis Herren with the marchers

Since The Times was probably not the newspaper of choice of many of the organisers, they had to make enquiries as to who Herren actually was, assuming that he would be an industrial or regional reporter! Herren's own parents had been unemployed and his daily reports were both detailed and thoughtful, giving a fine insight into the motives and backgrounds of the individual marchers, as the following extracts show:-

May 5th

"Presumably some will dismiss this march as a political stunt. Organised by the North West, West Midlands and South East Regions of the TUC, it has attracted some youngsters whose politics shade from pale pink to

deepest red. But the leaders are middle-aged trade union stalwarts, and they are well supported by the rank and file of many unions. Despite a CND group and a few punks, the response of the people watching them march past could not be mistaken. They clapped and the marchers clapped in return. Money, including pound notes, was stuffed into collection boxes."

May 7th

"Colin Barnett of the North West TUC, who organised the first section of the march, said he wanted the TUC's alternative economic strategy. He had bought 30,000 copies of the pamphlet and was willing to give a free copy to anybody who sent him a stamped addressed envelope and, if possible, a contribution to meet the expenses of the march...

May12th

"The Rev Ron Casson, the Rector of Stoke on Trent,...... said that the march had already achieved a great deal by making people think more seriously of the perils to the country posed by unemployment. Critics who belittle the march by making comparisons with unemployment between the wars were thoughtless and callous. Social security now cushioned the loss of income but it could not make up for the insecurity of skilled men who had lost their jobs. The involvement of the Church was important. How could it say that work makes men creative and enables them to serve God and then stand idly by when men were robbed of the opportunity to work?

May 15th

"...Derek Evans.....was more bitter than the other marchers, perhaps because a man, who thought he was a layabout, had told him to join the marines. 'Join the marines?' he repeated. 'Do you want two and a half million marines?'"

May 19th

"The rain was persistent and heavy as the Peoples March for Jobs moved down the Soho Road towards the City centre.......... A contingent from the local Indian Workers Association shouted 'Maggie, Maggie, out, out, out.' I had heard the cry many times before on this march; but never with such venom. The response from men and women lining the route was immediate. Sikh elders standing outside a yellow and blue temple filled a collecting box and blacks leaning from the windows of a garishly painted West Indian hotel waved and shouted."

May 21st

"......Mrs Thatcher's policies are said to be beginning to work in that some of the larger component companies have become more efficient and competitive by reducing their workforces. Which means, if temporarily, more unemployment. Very few of the marchers were prepared to accept her policies even if they can be seen to be working. They want jobs under almost any circumstances. This populist approach may be regrettable but is understandable. I doubt that I would be

147

an enthusiastic monetarist if I could not properly feed my children.........."

May 22nd

"The marchers had come a long way since they left Liverpool on May 1st. The new boots had finally broken in and they moved like seasoned campaigners, obedient to the friendly directions of the police and responding cheerfully to the clapping of passers-by."

May 27th

".............The Bull public house (Hemel Hempstead) had large signs taped to its doors stating 'no marchers'. I would have been tempted to tear them down if I had been a marcher but in the village hall nearby the welcome was as warm as in the north...".

May 30th

"The Peoples March for Jobs marched its last long mile yesterday and was given a warm reception by the Asian community of Southall. Samosas and other Indian dishes were provided at the community centre and, above the babble of Geordie, Scouse and Bangladeshi a clear Bombay Welsh voice cried, 'you are most welcome'."

As the 40,000 marchers converged on Trafalgar Square they found a further 50,000 waiting for them. A number of luminaries of the left addressed them .

Colin Barnett addressing the marchers in Trafalgar Square.

In the course of the March it appeared that the attitudes of the TUC hierarchy had mellowed somewhat. Perhaps they were genuinely moved by the March itself; perhaps they were shamed into it; or maybe they just did not want to be left out of the grand rally. Whatever their motives they certainly turned out at the finale. Indeed the Financial Times reported that,

"In the most thoughtful speech of the rally Mr Len Murray, TUC General Secretary, said the message of the need for change had to be delivered not just to the Government but to 'the employed men and women who are still indifferent to the plight of the unemployed'."

Whether many of those present appreciated the irony of this contribution is not reported.

Even the Daily Mail had to concede that the March had been *"impeccably organised"* and had *"symbolised the despair of Britain's genuinely unemployed people"*. However, it could not resist this, the only jarring note among all the national press on June 1st:-

"But it also became the Ascot of the Left Wing – attracting the type of fringe political groups which seize any opportunity to air their views. Yesterday's rally with labour moderates rubbing shoulders with members of the numerous fringe groups, spotlighted the disarray of the left of British politics."

It is not easy to assess the impact of the march. While it was taking place it certainly captured the popular imagination and elicited enormous public sympathy along the route. The final rally in Trafalgar Square provided an excellent platform for both Labour Party and TUC leaders to make broader political points and to bask in the reflected glory of the marchers. It also brought about a significant, if reluctant, change of heart on the part of the TUC hierarchy and the trade union movement generally so that, when a second march was organised the following year, it had official TUC backing.

Whether the marchers had any impact at all on the Conservative Government is extremely doubtful since they continued with their existing economic and industrial policies and, many respects, redoubled their efforts. Perhaps the marchers' objectives were simply too idealistic in that no one on the outside actually believed that full employment was either achievable or indeed in the national interest at that time. Perhaps the church leaders in Merseyside were right when they wrote at the beginning of the March,

"But we want to question the realism of the TUC's call to 'demand a return to full employment'. The Christian must insist on looking hard for where the truth lies in such a complex matter. To us it seems unlikely that with the introduction of new technology there will ever be a return to full employment in the old terms. Until we admit this, we cannot even begin to work out what needs to be done for the future."

One of the unintended, though perhaps inevitable consequences of the march and the role played in it by Colin Barnett was that, when he subsequently stood down as Regional Secretary of the TUC in 1985, he was replaced not by a volunteer, elected regionally, but by an appointee of the General Council. The degree of independence that he had exercised in going against the wishes of the General Council had not been forgotten and was clearly to be prevented in the future.

11. RETIREMENT

In March, 1984 Colin announced his retirement. Even after over 20 years his former colleagues still profess themselves puzzled by his decision. At the age of 55 he was considered to be an effective, shrewd and cunning operator and he worked longer hours than those working under him. His positions in NUPE, the TUC and the MSC had provided him with all the opportunities he had striven for to influence for the better the lives of the low-paid and unemployed in the north-west. In addition he was active in the peace movement and in anti-racism and still working for improved understanding between the peoples of Russia and Britain. His opponents still saw him as dangerous and formidable and, if his natural allies still regarded him as a maverick who could not be relied upon to toe any line about which he had reservations, they nonetheless respected his unbending principles and admired his courage and commitment. In short, he appeared to be in his pomp.

In fact he took his decision entirely because he knew that his physical mobility was deteriorating as result of his childhood illness and that if he were to continue in work he could not carry on at the same pace. Others have said that, if he had reduced his workload by a half, he would still have been working harder than most but that was not sufficient for him. Leading uncompromisingly from the front and dragging others in his wake was the only way that he knew how to operate.

It was not just his colleagues who were taken by surprise. The local and regional press thought there might be dark secrets that had prompted what appeared to be a sudden decision and Colin found himself having to explain in print why he had decided to retire. However, even at the point of departure, old habits died hard and he took the opportunity to espouse the causes dear to his heart.

The West Lancashire Evening Gazette reported,

"TUC North West Regional Secretary Colin Barnett is to retire early because of ill-health. The 55 year-old official of the public employees union NUPE will give up full-time employment in a month because of arthritis of the hip. ....

He said he regretted his enforced early retirement but was proud of the advances and achievements both NUPE and the TUC had made during his involvement.

"In NUPE we have made everybody aware of the importance of public services to the community and I think that these are now much more highly valued."

Mr Barnett said that one of his proudest achievements had been his part in organising the Peoples March for Jobs in 1981 but added he felt the TUC had missed an opportunity to press harder for action against the appalling unemployment problem.

He said that racism was still present among the working people and urged the union and Labour movements to continue with their education programmes to ensure any extreme right-wing champion could not attract popular support.

The Oldham Evening Chronicle described him as *"a controversial figure throughout his political and union career"* and said that he *"did not intend to disappear from public life"*. He went on to promise,

"I shall devote my time and energy to persuading the British people that Socialism has as much to do with a way of life as a political party. I will concentrate upon education in the cause of Socialism."

In the Liverpool Echo he warmed further to the theme:-

"I will continue my struggle to establish socialism in society as well as using my industrial knowledge lecturing.

I am a little sad to leave but I will not be disappearing from the public view altogether. I shall continue to be involved in the Labour movement and shall be involved in efforts to create a socialist society. The main achievement during my years with the trade union movement has been bringing the plight of the low-paid to public attention and getting the trade union movement to accept the concept of the basic minimum wage. My main concern as I leave is the continuing threat of racism in our society."

At national level it was the Daily Mail that over the years had consistently painted him as an unprincipled villain and they were not about to relent at the end of his career. They described how he had *"launched the second phase of his controversial career by sending out 20 letters to management consultants and university lecturers explaining how he can help them."*

He was then quoted as saying,

"They have a need for insights into trade union situations and I believe they could profit from what I know. I am well-known as an activist on behalf of NUPE and have been very outspoken. That will have to go. But I will argue in terms of the trade union movement as a whole. Over the years I have put forward views that have challenged many employers' assumptions – and that won't change. There is a need for mutual understanding but that doesn't make me a would-be lackey of the employers."

And just in case their readership had forgotten his reputation they reminded them of *"the would-be peacemaker's"* involvement in the Leonard Cheshire strike, the Dirty Jobs strike and his controversial divorce and re-marriage!

On the occasion of his retirement there was a large

gathering of NUPE colleagues, both locally and nationally, and it has been remarked upon by many who were present that it was the only occasion on which he had been seen to weep. In fact he simply sobbed. The general feeling was that, although he might not have been surprised to be admired or even feared, he was genuinely amazed to find that he was also held in deep affection and was very much moved at the idea. Indeed it is doubtful whether he had even considered whether or not he was liked – the cause was everything. But it was also clear that he was simply heart-broken to be leaving the job he loved and this was one disappointment from which he would not bounce back.

However, his disengagement was far from total. Indeed his *curriculum vitae* in retirement seems to have been almost as full as when he was in full-time employment. He established himself as a Business Consultant trading as C. M Barnett Associates, the title carefully disguising the fact that this was a one-man business. He continued as TUC Regional Secretary until a successor was found in 1985 and he remained a member of the Merseyside District Manpower Board until 1986.

Having served as a governor of the secondary school attended by his own children, he then joined the governing body of Broadway School, another secondary school in St Helens but serving a deprived area. Within a short time he was elected as Chairman. Subsequently the Headteacher, Martin Cox, was appointed as director of a newly established Education Action Zone in St Helens and, again, Colin was appointed as Chairman. He is remembered in this role for the insights he brought to the job and his purposeful and business-like chairmanship; and, since the new organisation frequently found itself in conflict with the St Helens LEA, for his fortitude and political skill.

In retirement he also continued as Employment Adviser to the Granada TV programme "This is Your Right" until 1989 and remained a member of the Industrial Tribunal in Manchester until 1999. He was a regular lecturer at the Manchester Business School and at other academic institutions in the region. He also became even more heavily involved in Anglo-Russian cultural and educational exchanges now that he had more time to devote to arranging them.

It was from the Russian connection that he came closest to an unlikely second career as an entrepreneur. His retirement coincided with the loosening of central bureaucratic controls in the former USSR, providing an outward-looking city such as St Petersburg with the opportunity to develop stronger trading links with the west. Colin had always had strong links with influential links in the city. He was also possessed of a fertile mind and enjoyed spotting opportunities for new developments.

As Hilary continued to work in a senior role in the NHS after Colin's retirement it was perhaps inevitable that he should turn his thoughts to hospitals and their potential to generate income for themselves. One of his ideas was to try to persuade Littlewoods, the low-cost, Liverpool retail group which enjoyed iconic status regionally, to open outlets in the larger Merseyside hospitals, thereby generating new business for the company and additional income for the hospitals. He carried out a certain amount of detailed research into the feasibility of such a scheme and arranged to meet Littlewoods' Finance Director to discuss it. In fact the Finance Director showed little interest in the proposal but that was not to be the end of their involvement with each other.

Colin had noticed that the Finance Director, who was incidentally of Bengali origin, had an impressive range of Russian crockery in his office. This prompted a discussion about Colin's Russian connections and, within ten minutes, he had been appointed as an adviser to the company for a fee of £1000 per month because, unknown to him, Littlewoods were interested in expanding their interests into post-Perestroika Russia and felt that Colin's contacts and his knowledge of the country could be of value to them.

And so it proved. As Communism's hold on Russian life weakened Colin was able to introduce Littlewoods' representatives to apparatchiks of the former regime and, through these contacts, the company was quite swiftly able to establish itself in small retail units in some of the larger department stores in Leningrad. Their goods proved popular with their Russia customers and their prices were reasonably affordable. They hired staff who had useful contacts, including a bizarre Afghan character who had been a KGB agent and who insisted on the protection of an unpleasant-looking rottweiller.

However, the company had ambitions in Russia which extended beyond what Colin thought sensible. Firstly they insisted on opening their own large stores similar to those operating in Britain without first making a sufficiently detailed analysis of what the embryonic Russian market would bear. But, more crucially, they aspired to hold a place in the Russian high streets on a par with that enjoyed by Marks and Spencer in Britain. Colin argued with them that the attraction of Littlewoods to Russians who visited Merseyside was their low prices; Russian visitors seldom sought out Marks and Spencer simply because their prices were higher than they could afford. He felt that they were throwing away what natural advantages they had in favour of a climb up-market that was doomed to failure. In the event he was proved correct and Littlewoods had to scale down their Russian operations and eventually closed the business there. Another retail chain which suffered a similar fate was Mothercare, which seems to have proved too expensive for the average Russian shopper, while the more affluent ones were already travelling more easily to the west and were therefore able to enjoy their Mothercare shopping throughout Western Europe.

Other companies sought Colin out for advice and contacts in the former Soviet Union and in return he organised fact-finding trips and introductions. However, he was also approached with proposals with which he was far less comfortable. For example, many affluent Russian women seeking the opportunity to have their babies in Britain but were frustrated in this because British airlines refused to carry heavily pregnant passengers. Aeroflot were less squeamish, however, and Colin was asked if he would be interested in taking on responsibility for the practical arrangements – an approach he had little difficulty in rejecting. He was even asked if he would organise a marriage agency in Britain for Russian girls seeking a legal means of emigrating to Britain. Again he declined.

One initiative that he did take up was to act as an agent for Russian doctors seeking to extend their experience in Britain. For a number of years he had arranged exchange visits and home-stays for Russian medical staff as part of his efforts to establish better cultural links between the two countries and he saw the new circumstances as an opportunity to extend these arrangements. However, he was shaken to discover that from the first group of Russian doctors that he brought to Britain no less than four defected. Clearly that had been far from his intention.

Gradually the contacts that he had made over the years became less useful; new men were establishing their influence in Russia and more formal organisations were set up to promote trade between Britain and Russia, which made Colin's role far less crucial. He also found that international travel became more and more difficult for him physically. However, for a time he had enjoyed a prominent position as a commercial intermediary and had managed to supplement his pension quite lucratively in the process. If that seems on the face of it in any way to have compromised the socialist ideals he had espoused all his life, it also has to be seen in the context of a long-term commitment to Anglo-Russian understanding. He might argue that it was simply that his aspirations were now being shared by many who would have vilified him for them a decade earlier.

As time passed and Hilary too retired from her role in the NHS in Merseyside, they finally left the north-west conurbation that had occupied their working lives and settled in Sedbergh, in south Cumbria, where they had had a weekend home for a number of years. Physical handicaps began to take their toll on Colin but he remains deeply interested in political and world affairs as well as community life in Sedbergh. He is unrepentant about any of the positions he adopted during his active political life, although in some cases he can be persuaded to see a few more shades of grey in what was previously a predominantly black and white view of the world. However, this did not deter him from resigning from the Labour Party after over 50 years, out of a deep distaste for the brand of socialism espoused by Tony Blair and New Labour. Perhaps the only surprise is that it took so long.

EPILOGUE

In compiling this account of Colin Barnett's life I have been fascinated to try to peel back its layers of complexity. I have seen a man of steadfast, even unbending, political beliefs. I can attest to his unwavering dedication to the interests of the low-paid and unemployed and to his delight to have witnessed in his life-time the adoption of a national minimum wage that he and his union fought so hard to achieve in the face of the trade union establishment's determination to thwart it. Yet, during the "Dirty Jobs" strike, a former colleague from the LSE in the 1950s was quoted in the press as being astonished at his transformation over 25 years from a rather earnest, compassionate, young Christian into the ruthless campaigner who asserted that in denying patients hospital treatment, leaving rubbish to pile up in the streets and parks and postponing funerals he was choosing the "lesser of two evils". It was suggested that his altruism had become far more selective over the years.

I have been impressed by the courage of a man with life-long physical difficulties whose hatred of racism led him to defy threats to his life in order to challenge the influence of the National Front and other racist groups. I have followed too his constant support for the Peace Movement and for better Anglo-Russian understanding at a time when to hold such views was seen as something akin to treason. In none of these beliefs has he wavered. As one who has changed his views on so many important issues over the years I confess that I still have difficulty in understanding how a man's mental framework can remain so untroubled by political doubt.

However, there is also the man of religion, on an endless and ultimately unsuccessful quest for the same certainty on the spiritual front that he has enjoyed in his secular beliefs. From potential Anglican priest to occasional visitor to Quaker meetings has indeed been a long and perhaps unrewarding journey. But in the process he has become widely read and articulate in argument. It would be difficult to tell that his formal education stopped at the age of sixteen.

Colin the man is now far more heavily affected by his physical incapacity and he tires quickly. He is still more than ready to give advice and unqualified support to anyone who needs it but his memory for detail is not quite as sharp it was. It is therefore not immediately apparent in a first meeting why he once generated such panic among both his opponents and his allies, almost in equal measure. I hope that this memoir will go some way to providing an explanation.

INDEX

THE AUTHOR

Ray Marriott was born in 1946 in Nottinghamshire. He read Modern History at Keble College, Oxford and, after teaching at Leeds Grammar School, entered local government as an education officer. He worked for North Yorkshire, Humberside, Cumbria and Lancashire County Councils and now lives in retirement in the Yorkshire Dales. He is married to Glenys and has three children and two grandchildren. This is his first book.